Egyptian Mythology

An Enthralling Overview of Egyptian Myths, Gods, and Goddesses

Free limited time bonus

Stop for a moment. We have a free bonus set up for you. The problem is this: we forget 90% of everything that we read after 7 days. Crazy fact, right? Here's the solution: we've created a printable, 1-page pdf summary for this book that you're reading now. All you have to do to get your free pdf summary is to go to the following website: **https://livetolearn.lpages.co/enthrallinghistory/**

Once you do, it will be intuitive. Enjoy, and thank you!

We forget 90% of everything that we've read in 7 days...

Get the free printable pdf summary of the book you've read AND much, much more... shhhh...

Enter Your Most Frequently Used Email to Get Started

DOWNLOAD FREE PDF SUMMARY

© Enthralling History

Contents

INTRODUCTION...1

PART ONE: COSMOLOGY...4

    CHAPTER 1 - THE CREATION MYTHS 5

    CHAPTER 2 - THE SHAPE OF THE WORLD AND MA'AT............. 16

    CHAPTER 3 - THE DUAT AND THE AFTERLIFE 23

PART TWO: MYTHS AND LEGENDS.. 30

    CHAPTER 4 - RA AND APOPHIS 31

    CHAPTER 5 - THE OSIRIS MYTH 36

    CHAPTER 6 - TIME AND THE END OF TIMES 44

    CHAPTER 7 - THE GOLDEN LOTUS.. 56

    CHAPTER 8 - THE GREEK PRINCESS 61

    CHAPTER 9 - THE TREASURE THIEF.. 73

    CHAPTER 10 - THE TALE OF HATSHEPSUT 81

    CHAPTER 11 - THE DOOMED PRINCE 89

    CHAPTER 12 - THE TWO BROTHERS.................................... 93

    CHAPTER 13 - ISIS AND THE SEVEN SCORPIONS 98

    CHAPTER 14 - THE PRINCE AND THE SPHINX............................ 101

    CHAPTER 15- THE ADVENTURES OF SINUHE............................ 106

PART THREE: GODS AND GODDESSES 112

    CHAPTER 16- AMUN-RA.. 113

    CHAPTER 17 - ISIS, OSIRIS, AND HORUS 120

CHAPTER 18 – SET AND NEPHTHYS 130

CHAPTER 19 – ANUBIS AND THOTH 141

CHAPTER 20 – HATHOR AND BASTET 150

PART FOUR: THE SACRED BOOKS 159

CHAPTER 21 – THE COFFIN TEXTS AND THE BOOK OF
THE DEAD 160

CHAPTER 22 – THE BOOKS OF CAVERNS, GATES, AND
THE HEAVENLY COW 167

CONCLUSION 177

HERE'S ANOTHER BOOK BY ENTHRALLING HISTORY THAT
YOU MIGHT LIKE 179

FREE LIMITED TIME BONUS 180

BIBLIOGRAPHY 181

Introduction

Unraveling the mysteries of our existence is one of man's greatest accomplishments. The knowledge we have was made ours by searching, finding, and exploring the world that existed thousands of years before us. Egyptian mythology brings the vivid details of the very distant past to us, and as you are about to discover, there is so much to learn!

Ancient Egypt is synonymous with massive pyramids, the worship of the sun, and their plethora of gods and goddesses. On every page of this book, you will find the multiple, exciting perspectives of their stories. But first, how about getting familiar with some Egyptian mythology lingo?

- **ASPECT:** This seems like a regular word, but watch out for how it is used in ancient mythology, especially when referring to the gods. An "aspect" of a god or goddess means a version of them. If there is one thing to note in advance about the gods and goddesses in Egyptian mythology, it is their ability to shapeshift or manifest in diverse forms. These forms could be animals, inanimate objects, or a separate god altogether. A god could transform into any of these forms or extract a separate god from himself.

- **AMULET:** Amulets are manmade objects or tokens believed to ward off evil. They could be ornaments, charms, crests, jewelry, a small piece of paper with spells written on it, or objects from nature, like claws or shells. An amulet is typically wearable and portable.

- **ANKH:** In nearly every picture of an Egyptian god or goddess, you will see them holding a key-like hook in one hand. This hook is called an ankh, and it was a divine symbol representing the immortality of the gods.

- **DYNASTY:** This was the collective term used to describe pharaohs from the same family line. The end of a dynasty was when a pharaoh from another royal family ascended to the throne. Ancient Egypt had over thirty dynasties, including those of the Greeks and Romans.

- **MIDDLE KINGDOM:** Although the Middle Kingdom is not mentioned very much in this book, it was an era of ancient Egypt. It came between the Old Kingdom and the New Kingdom. The years vary from one history book to another, but a convenient timeline is between c. 2030 BCE and 1640 BCE. Some history textbooks do not acknowledge the Middle Kingdom. Instead, they fuse it with the New Kingdom. An event used to demarcate the Middle Kingdom from the New Kingdom is the Hyksos invasion of Egypt around 1638 BCE, as it caused great political instability.

- **NEW KINGDOM:** The New Kingdom is also regarded as the golden age of ancient Egypt. After getting their land back from the invading foreigners, the pharaohs worked hard to return the nation to its former glory. Impressive structures, magnificent statues, and other antique masterpieces come from this era. Again, the dates differ, but the general consensus is that the New Kingdom typically dates between c. 1550 BCE and 1077 BCE.

- **OLD KINGDOM:** It is all in the name. The Old Kingdom of ancient Egypt is the time before the Middle and New Kingdom eras, dating between c. 2700 BCE and 2200 BCE. At this time, Egypt existed as two regions: Upper and Lower Egypt. The Old Kingdom was also the era of the pyramids. Pharaohs in this era had tall pyramids built to commemorate their reign and serve as royal tombs. The famous Sphinx of Giza was also built in the Old Kingdom era.

- **PAPYRUS:** This was thick ancient Egyptian paper used as early as the Predynastic era of Egypt. It is named after the plant it was made from. If you lived back then, you could find papyrus in abundance around the Nile River.

- **PRIMEVAL/PRIMORDIAL:** This is used to refer to the mythical timeline of Egypt. It is the oldest, earliest era in Egypt, dating from the creation of the world to the reign of the gods. No years or figures are used to describe this era.

- **PTOLEMAIC ERA:** This is the time after the New Kingdom era when Egypt was invaded and occupied by the Macedonians. This era is named after Ptolemy I, a Macedonian general who served Alexander the Great. By 305 BCE, Ptolemy had defeated anyone with claims to the throne and became the king of Egypt. About 275 years after, Egypt was annexed into the Roman Empire, marking the end of this era. In this book, Egypt during this time is described as Graeco-Roman Egypt. Now that you are ready, it is time to dive in! We begin with the earliest of times in Egyptian mythology and the first story in its chronology: the creation of the world.

Part One: Cosmology

Chapter 1 – The Creation Myths

Of all the creation stories out there, those from ancient Egypt are some of the most intriguing. Stories of where elements of nature and living creatures come from are a part of nearly every ancient civilization in history. The creation of the world has been recounted by many cultures. What you are bound to notice first is that they all allude to chaos or a void before the establishment of the natural order.

The Egyptian creation myths, in all their dynamism, are not exempt from this.

Sometimes, the word "myth" is ascribed to falsehood or uncertainty, but the Egyptians believed every creation myth to be profoundly true. You may read of Egyptian creation myths or any creation myth at all as "cosmological myths" in some texts. It is a synonym. Cosmology studies the totality of the universe, from the origin to its evolution to its eventual fate.

Sources of Egyptian Creation Myths

The multi-versioned Egyptian stories of creation come to us from ancient hieroglyphic compilations from the Old Kingdom, spanning from around 2700 BCE to 2200 BCE.

The Egyptians are world-famous for their elaborate funerals and gravesites. Pharaohs from the Old and Middle Kingdoms were buried in pyramids, with stories from their time told on the tomb walls. These are called Pyramid Texts.

Pyramid text on the tomb walls of Pharaoh Teti of the Sixth Dynasty.
Credit: Leon petrosyan, CC BY-SA 4.0 https://creativecommons.org/licenses/by-sa/4.0 via Wikimedia Commons https://commons.wikimedia.org/wiki/File:In_ther_pyramid_of_Teti_1.jpg

A pyramid was much roomier than your average tomb, and the Egyptians believed that there was no better way to send off their kings to have a blessed afterlife. Pyramids typically had stairs that would lead the deceased king up to the sky (or the sun), guided by protective texts and spells on the walls. These were known as funerary texts. Thousands of years later, multiple excavations of these ancient pyramids practically gifted the world with most of the profound knowledge that exists today about Egyptian creation myths.

Ancient temples were another prominent source. The ancient Egyptians took to carving their stories on a temple's stone walls and ceiling. Perhaps they foresaw the destruction of important religious documents in the soon-to-come conflict-ridden transition of Egypt from polytheistic paganism to Christianity. During this time, the

Christians destroyed many documented texts about Egyptian gods and goddesses.

Despite the eventuality of this conversion, creation myths recorded on papyrus paper survived. Such documents, including religious texts written by priests, spell books compiled by magicians, and medical journals written by physicians from the ancient era, have proven to be valuable sources of information about the creation myths and other information about Egypt. They highlight the names of the gods responsible for protection and healing, as well as their roles in creating the world.

Fascinatingly, classical Greek authors also did their bit in making Egyptian creation myths world famous. You probably know of names like Herodotus, Plutarch, and maybe even Diodorus. However, none of these men could speak Egyptian to save their lives, but they proved that a curious mind truly distinguished what made someone an ardent seeker of knowledge.

Their goal was to educate a Greek audience with foreign stories and enrich the Greek culture. But due to the language barrier, these classical authors were at the mercy of interpreters. They relied on the interpreters to read the Egyptian scrolls and carvings on the walls or speak with the Egyptian custodians of knowledge, the priests. Eventually, Greek authors recorded the Egyptian stories based on what they had gleaned from these interpreters. You can imagine that these accounts were imbued with personal and cultural biases. The essence of some stories was lost or diluted in the translation process, resulting in a wide range of differences from the local Egyptian versions. The classical Greek authors could have cared less about these distortions, especially since their accounts practically renamed some of the Egyptian gods. For example, the Egyptian god Amun became Zeus-Ammon (arguably different from Zeus), the Egyptian god Horus was identified with Apollo, and Thoth was combined with the Greek god Hermes.

It seemed as though the classical authors from Greece were not as interested in popularizing the Egyptian creation myths as they were in offering their fellow Greeks a form of entertainment. Barring the inherent inconsistencies, the written stories of classical Greek authors about Egyptian creation myths, which were eventually integrated into ancient Greek culture, have proven to be another key historical source.

Last but certainly not least on the list of sources is word of mouth. This source has been criticized as very unreliable, but Egyptians have always taken pride in telling stories of old. Ancient pharaohs were famed for being excellent storytellers, an ability they shared with their children. Their folktales lauded the exploits of Atum (or Ra) and spoke of the wisdom of Osiris and the beauty of Nut, the sky above them. No doubt, such fervent storytellers would have many versions of a single story, which depended on location and religious perspective. However, these stories had some common ground. Rather than dwell on the inconsistencies of these versions, it is best to think of such dynamic awareness of the universe and its origin as an example of a sophisticated culture.

There is indeed no single tomb, temple, book, or document that paints a whole picture of Egypt's creation myths, but what is mythology without some mystery? After all, the archaeological efforts throughout the years are just enough to put pen to paper.

Accounts of Egyptian Creation Myths

A map of ancient Egypt.
Credit: Jeff Dahl, CC BY-SA 4.0 https://creativecommons.org/licenses/by-sa/4.0 via Wikimedia Commons; https://commons.wikimedia.org/wiki/File:Ancient_Egypt_map-en.svg

There are four prominent creation stories, which come from four different cities in Egypt. The first one and arguably the most popular is from the ancient city of Heliopolis. The story begins with our beloved universe as nothing but a chaotic, directionless expanse of water known as Nun.

Heliopolis

It is difficult to imagine what nothingness looks like, but a few decent attempts have been made at its portrayal. Nun is the name given to the universe's form before creation, and it bore much semblance to a vast turbulent ocean. It reached everywhere yet went nowhere. There was no night or day, and the only being existent inside the water was a motionless god.

His name was Atum (or Ra in some texts).

Atum must have spent eons in his inert solitude, enough to long for companionship. In time, he decided to put an end to his loneliness. Atum emerged from Nun on a cone-shaped mystical stone called Benben, and in some other accounts, Atum emerged by calling out his own name. As an accessory to his peculiar nature, the god Atum had male and female elements within his being. This enabled him to procreate with himself. He birthed two children: Shu and Tefnut.

Ennead: A Divine Genealogy

Of course, there are variations within our Heliopolitan story as to how Atum conceived his offspring. While some traditions imply an act similar to masturbation, others suggest that Atum mated with his own shadow. Another account tells us that the god Atum sneezed out Shu and spat out Tefnut and that their names are onomatopoeic puns to represent how they were born.

These unique accounts, despite their divergence, unanimously agree that the god Atum was the father of Shu and Tefnut. Shu became the god of air, and his sister Tefnut became the goddess of moisture—the two foundational elements of nature. Together, the twins would embark on a journey to discover their purpose and how to fulfill it.

Atum was unhappy to send his children off into a world pervaded by abysmal darkness and uncertainty, but he could not keep them satisfying their curiosities. So, away they went, but Shu and Tefnut were barely gone before Atum realized that his purpose for creating his children had been defeated.

He was once again lonely.

Desperate for their safety, the god Atum took a part of himself, his eye, and sent it on an important mission to find his tarrying children. Atum's eye, also known as the Eye of Ra, traversed the void until Shu and Tefnut were found and reunited with their father.

Atum received his children with tears of joy. Every teardrop that plopped down from his eyes transformed into a living creature—the first generation of mankind to inhabit a new world.

However, there remained a small challenge. The waters of Nun were not conducive for Atum's latest creation. They needed a place to call home for themselves, somewhere their children could grow. In this dilemma, Shu and Tefnut discovered the purpose they had previously ventured wide and far to find.

The union of Shu and Tefnut birthed the second generation in divinity: the god of the earth, Geb, and the goddess of the sky, Nut. Geb is portrayed in art as a green-skinned man who typically holds up a woman, who is believed to be his sister, Nut. Beautiful Nut arches above her brother, and her body is home to bright glowing dots (stars). It was also believed that Nut swallowed the sun every night and had it reborn to mark the beginning of a new day.

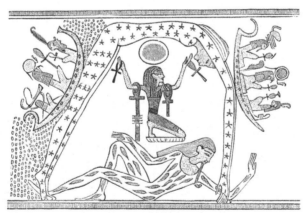

A portrayal of Nut stretching over her brother Geb.
https://commons.wikimedia.org/wiki/File:PSM_V10_D564_Egyptian_representation_of_heaven_and
_earth.jpg

Due to sharing such an intimate coexistence, Geb and Nut quickly fell in love with each other, but their father, Shu, disapproved; some believe he might have been jealous of the union. As a consequence, Shu separated the two, forcing them to exist without the other. Ancient Egyptians believed that this is why the earth and sky are parallel elements of nature to this day.

Heartbroken, Geb shed tears of sadness since he could not live with his true love. The Egyptians believed this was where rain and oceans came from.

Before Nut's separation from Geb, she had birthed four children: Osiris, Isis, Set, and Nephthys. A few Egyptian traditions include a fifth child named Horus, but most name Horus as the son of Osiris and Isis, not their brother. A third version alludes to the existence of both: Horus the Elder as their brother and Horus the Younger as their son.

The four (or five) children of Geb and Nut would represent the forces of nature and shape mankind's journey on the earth in stages.

So, from Atum (Ra), the sun god and father of all creation, came Shu and Tefnut; from Shu and Tefnut came Geb and Nut; and from Geb and Nut came four gods and goddesses: Osiris, Isis, Set, and Nephthys.

Together, these nine gods are revered as the Great Ennead of Heliopolis.

Hermopolis

The Hermopolitan version of creation is the oldest, and it does not center around nine gods but eight: the sacred Ogdoad.

The Ogdoad of Hermopolis carved on the wall of a tomb in Deir el-Medina.
SFEC_2009_POT-0008.JPG: S F-E-Cameronderivative work: JMCCl, CC BY-SA 3.0
https://creativecommons.org/licenses/by-sa/3.0 via Wikimedia Commons;
https://commons.wikimedia.org/wiki/File:Ogdoad_-_The_Place_of_Truth_-_Deir_el_Medina.jpg

Before the creation of life, these divine beings existed as elements that characterized the world: utter darkness, chaotic waters, mystery, and infinity.

These eight gods were in four pairs, one male and one female. You will find that the male gods had frog heads, while their female counterparts had the heads of serpents. Their names were Nun (or Nu) and Naunet, Hah and Hauhet, Kek and Kauket, and Amun and Amaunet.

Together, they sailed upon the primeval waters that would become a new world. The Hermopolitan creation myth tells of the interaction between these eight gods and their energies, which resulted in a massive explosion; today, it is what scientists call the Big Bang. Consequently, a primordial mound (possibly the Benben) emerged from the waters. This marked the beginning of the golden age on Earth, with the Ogdoad as rulers.

The Four-Way Street

The Hermopolitan creation myth, like that of Heliopolis, has multiple subplots, which are all connected to the Ogdoad. First, a cosmic egg was the source of the universe and everything within it. Some traditions say that the egg was created by the gods themselves, while others say that it was laid by a primeval goose called the Gengen Wer (the Great Cackler), an aspect of the gods Amun and Geb. From this egg came the god Ra (or Atum), who began creating the world.

Another variation of that story involves a mystical lotus that emerged from the primeval waters. This lotus had petals that slowly opened and birthed a bird of light, representing Ra, who began the creation of the world. The third account agrees that the lotus came out of the waters, but instead of Ra, a scarab beetle emerged from the lotus when it opened. It shone as bright as the sun, marking the first sunrise. In some mythological versions, this scarab beetle transformed into a boy named Nefertum. His tears were what created the first human beings to ever walk the earth.

The fourth Hermopolitan version of creation holds that the world came from neither a lotus nor a celestial goose but from an egg laid by a sacred bird known as an ibis. This ibis was Thoth, the god of writing, science, and magic.

The Hermopolitans proudly assert that their creation stories are the oldest since they account for the origin of Ra, the source of the universe. According to them, the god Ra (or Atum) had not just come into existence. He was a creation of the eight gods known as the Ogdoad.

Thebes and Memphis

Many pantheons in ancient Thebes had carvings and statues of Amun, one of the gods in the Ogdoad. This god was worshiped in Thebes as a supreme being and the most important god when it came to creation. The Thebans believed that other gods were the creation of Amun and that the world would not exist without him. He created the goose (the Great Cackler) that broke the void of the primeval waters and summoned the primeval mound (or stone) that would house Atum.

The worshipers of Amun also believed that Thebes, the mighty capital city of Egypt in the 11th century BCE, was founded by Amun, along with the rest of the world. When Thebes rose to prominence in Egypt, Amun became a superior god.

In Memphis, another ancient Egyptian city, a deity named Ptah, the god of crafts and architecture, is believed to have used his expertise in divine speech to form the gods and the world. He was also revered as the protector of what he had created, and he was the only god who had not been created by another.

Wildly varying as these creation stories from ancient Egypt seemed, they share a few fascinating similarities. First is the belief that the world was created by gods, supernatural beings who either created themselves or came into existence through extraordinary means.

Second is the belief that before creation, the universe existed as a watery void. This is symbolic of a state of chaos, emptiness, and the lack of order—that is, until the gods emerge and save the day. The writers of these myths remain to be discovered, but what is certain is that these creation stories have greatly shaped Egyptian culture, both back then and today.

Chapter 2 – The Shape of the World and Ma'at

Curiosity is perhaps humanity's greatest gift; otherwise, how would knowledge ever come to us?

The world has been home to humankind for many eons, and as inhabitants of a truly complex environment, the onus of finding the truth has been passed down from one generation to the next. Ancient Egypt is famed for being a center of art, culture, and natural science, which includes cosmology, in which people seek the meaning of the world they live in.

Modern scientific information and technologies were nonexistent at the time, so the Egyptians who sought such knowledge of the universe relied heavily on the supernatural. Gods and goddesses had to have had a hand in how the universe was structured. They also had a hand in the routines of nature, such as dawn and dusk, rain and drought, and wind and storms. Most significant of all, the gods designed the shape of the world.

If you visited the most revered scientists in ancient Egypt, who typically doubled as priests, they would tell you that the earth was flat and oval-shaped. This is evident in the journey of Ra to the underworld, a journey he took every day. It is often described as a descent. This shows the Egyptians thought there was a slope or curve at the edge of the earth from one realm to the other. After his all-night sojourn, the sun god would rise again on the other side, which would be referred to as an ascent.

As you will recall in the Heliopolitan creation myth, the grandchildren of Ra, Geb and Nut, were connected. You will also recall that the goddess Nut is portrayed as a naked woman arched over her brother Geb. She represents the sky (or heavens), through which Ra travels during the daytime.

The arch of Nut speaks to the oval shape theory that ancient Egyptians held. The other half of the oval was the underworld (also known as the Duat), completing a flat oval.

Ma'at: The Order of the World

The world did not just come to be. It had taken the hand of the divine Amun, who turned the desolate waters of Nun into a beautiful home for living creatures of all kinds. With all that work came Ma'at, the order of the universe. Ma'at is a core aspect of Egyptian mythology, cutting across the lives of the gods and their relationship with the mortals.

The exact beginning of Ma'at was creation, and thenceforth, every new king of Egypt had a duty to maintain it. Ma'at would also influence the fate of each soul in the afterlife. Essentially, Ma'at cut across all spheres of existence for both mortals and immortals as a "what" and a "who."

Ma'at: The "What"

First, ancient Egyptian mythology presents Ma'at as a principle, an idea or concept of justice, fairness, order, and harmony. The name itself means "that which is straight." When Amun (or Ra) created the world, his intention was companionship and harmony. The chaotic waters of Nun had long existed, and the creator yearned for peace.

Through the power of divine magic called *heka*, the world was brought to order. The first batch of people who occupied the earth upheld it in honor of their creator. Ancient Egyptians believed that to remain in line with Ma'at, every human had a duty to themself, their fellow humans, their creator, and the earth. Some of these duties, such as humility, self-control, and wisdom, were outlined by an ancient Egyptian vizier named Ptahhotep in his book titled *The Maxims of Ptahhotep*.

These duties were to be followed on the basis of social class, age, and gender. Times and seasons were also associated with Ma'at. Every year, there was a time when the Nile River would flood and a time when it would pull back. This was the order of things, and disruptions in these natural processes were deemed to be a sign of chaos or the anger of the gods. The ascension of a new king was also part of Ma'at.

After the era of being ruled by the gods, Egypt was ruled by men. These men stood as representatives of the gods on Earth, and after the demise of a king, another had to be enthroned to preserve Ma'at. Unrighteous kings would bring misfortune upon the land of Egypt and be condemned to eternal suffering in the afterlife after they died. Ma'at also represented the law but in a more natural and spiritual than legal sense. The kings of Egypt were expected to be models of these laws.

In Egyptian mythology, the principles of justice and order (Ma'at) apply to not just Egypt but also to every nation on the earth. In the ages to come, principles similar to those of Ma'at from other nations would be established in Egypt.

Ma'at: The Who

Reconstructed painting of Ma'at. *Credit: TYalaA, CC BY-SA 4.0*
https://creativecommons.org/licenses/by-sa/4.0 via Wikimedia Commons;
https://commons.wikimedia.org/wiki/File:Goddess_Ma%27at_or_Maat_of_Ancient_Egypt_-
_reconstructed.png

In images, Ma'at appears as a beautiful goddess with golden wings, holding an ankh and scepter and wearing an ostrich-feathered headdress. She was born from Amun (Ra) by the power of *heka* (magic) when the world was created.

Ma'at was the reason why the world continued on an orderly path after creation, as all elements of nature were in their place and served their ordained purpose. This goddess was an embodiment of harmony, justice, and continuity. She was the reason why the day was day, the night was night, the sky was the sky, and the earth was the earth as they had been created. Astronomers in ancient Egypt believed that the stars in the night sky chartered their course at the whims of Ma'at.

Of all the goddesses in the ancient Egyptian pantheon, Ma'at had a distinctive nature. She was not a protagonist in any myth like Isis or Hathor. Instead, she was a manifestation of an idea. The people practiced her as a principle rather than worship her as a deity. She represented rules that had to be obeyed rather than a figure who had to be bowed to.

The influence of Ma'at was so ingrained in the structure of Egypt that she was the basis of education. Apart from the pharaoh, scholars, scribes, and other members of the literate elite in Egypt, there were custodians of the knowledge of Ma'at. These bureaucrats were men of high standing in society who worshiped Ma'at alongside her husband Thoth, the god of wisdom.

The scribes were also in charge of educating the people on how to live their lives in accordance with the world order through oral traditions and instructional texts. One of the most famous scribes to write an instructional text in Egypt was Amenemope. His book, titled *Instruction of Amenemope*, was an advanced version of *The Maxims of Ptahhotep*, which had been written many years before Amenemope was born. During the Twentieth Dynasty of ancient Egypt, Amenemope's book became a manual for pleasing the goddess Ma'at.

The book opened by exhorting the people to obedience and a righteous interpretation of his words. It also spoke of the rewards of putting his instructions into practice:

"If you spend a lifetime with these things in your heart,

You will find it good fortune;

You will discover my words to be a treasure house of life,

And your body will flourish upon earth."

Next, the book warned against the ill-treatment of the poor, disrespect for elders, and engaging in shady business. These constituted some of the worst vices in ancient Egypt and were condemned as threats to the preservation of Ma'at.

Amenemope's book hinged largely on the topic of self-control and restraint in the face of provocation. By exhorting the people not to "quarrel with the argumentative man," to "proceed cautiously before an opponent," and to leave such people to themselves, he portrayed compliant people as being worthy examples to their children.

Public behavior and conduct were other topics that the people received clear instructions about in Amenemope's book. In places of worship, they were to be sober and silent. Since land matters were a common source of dispute in antiquity, Amenemope's book spoke against greed and altering land boundaries to accrue ill-gotten wealth or for cultivation:

"And receive the bread from your own threshing floor:

Better is the bushel which God gives you

Than five thousand deceitfully gotten."

Ensuing chapters condemned gluttony among masters and servants and bribery among government officials. He also spoke of Thoth's punishment reserved for corrupt scribes.

"The Ape [Thoth] rests [in] the temple of Khmun,

While his eye travels around the Two Lands;

If he sees one who sins with his finger [that is, a false scribe],

he takes away his provisions by the flood.

As for a scribe who sins with his finger,

His son shall not be enrolled."

Arrogance, trouble-mongering, false witnesses, and mud-slinging were also vehemently rebuked, especially since they were (and still are) common in the practice of law.

The exceptional writing abilities of scribes in antiquity made the principles of Ma'at easily understood and practicable to the people.

Even though the goddess Ma'at had no temples of her own like other goddesses, she was more important than most. Some might argue that she was the most important of all. She represented life itself, and she was omnipresent. Kings offered prayers to her to help them preserve order, and the people prayed for the same in their homes and on the streets. Every mortal in Egypt worshiped her by living their lives, and her influence remained intact for many generations.

In the afterlife, the Egyptians believed that every man's heart would be weighed against Ma'at to determine how much they complied with the principles of justice. This test would take place in the Duat, the famous underworld and the land of the dead.

Chapter 3 – The Duat and the Afterlife

The Duat, also known as the underworld or Tuat, was the home of the dead. You can picture it as a dark, chilly place where droves of souls desperately awaited the arrival of Ra to revitalize them, but there was more to it than that. Ironic as it sounds, although the Duat was the "land of the dead," it was a hive of activity.

As staunch believers in life after death, the people of ancient Egypt called the Duat a soul's eternal home, meaning that one would find many souls there. There were also mythical creatures, gods, goddesses, demons, and spirits, each with roles to play.

In earlier texts, the Duat was portrayed as a celestial heaven rather than an "underworld." This was because the pharaohs who died and went to the Duat were said to have gone up to the sky as stars or became part of the sun, which traveled each day through the body of the sky goddess Nut. This makes the concept of the Duat a tad ambiguous, considering that the sky is located above the earth and not under it. Subsequently, during the Middle Kingdom, the Duat became popularized as an underworld where all humans would spend eternity.

The Duat is represented in hieroglyphic texts as a star in a circle, which possibly alludes to its multiple sub-realms. There was the realm where souls were judged, another realm where gods and goddesses lived, another realm where men who had upheld Ma'at would live, and a realm for the unjust. Thus, heaven and hell were in one place, just in different locations.

Geographically, the underworld had features that were recognizable to the souls that called it home. This included lakes and oceans with boats for souls to travel in, as well as mountains and hills. Walls made of iron, lakes of fire, and turquoise trees were slightly out of the ordinary, but the underworld struck an expected balance between normal and spectral.

The Duat: The Land of the Dead

A soul's journey into the Duat began with death.

After death, a person would be embalmed and mummified. During this process, all the internal organs in the corpse would be removed, leaving only the heart in its place. This was because the heart would be needed in the Duat.

Mummification was an important practice in ancient Egypt. It involved the removal of all moisture from a corpse, as it could cause decay. This practice was aimed at preserving much of the deceased's physical form. Although it was the soul of a person that transitioned to the Egyptian afterlife, the physical body was an equally important vessel. This vessel would convey the soul to the gates of the Duat. If the body was broken or rotten, the spirit could get lost.

It is important to emphasize that for the better part of the Old Kingdom, only pharaohs could aspire to find paradise in the afterlife. Subsequently, the people came to the knowledge that even commoners had a place in the afterlife if they were willing to do what it took. Mummification was an expensive process that was not affordable for most commoners, but the practice of drying out a corpse in the desert sun for over seventy days worked as well.

While men were more commonly mummified, noblewomen who could afford the process were mummified too. Fascinatingly, a well-preserved mummy of a pregnant woman from the 1ˢᵗ century BCE was unearthed in the royal tombs of Luxor in 2018.

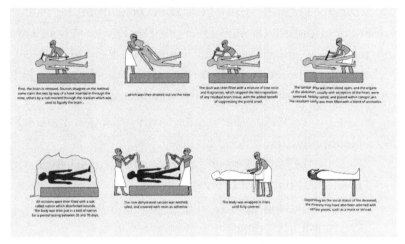

The process of mummification.
Credit: SimplisticReps, CC BY-SA 4.0 https://creativecommons.org/licenses/by-sa/4.0 via Wikimedia Commons; https://commons.wikimedia.org/wiki/File:Mummification_simple.png

The dead were typically buried on the west bank of the Nile River, as it was believed to be the best route to the underworld. Funeral rites included invoking guardian gods and goddesses to assist the soul to the underworld. Apart from magic spells and incantations, these invocations involved such things as burying amulets, figurines, and statues of protection with the deceased.

Then, the deceased would reawaken in the Duat. The Duat was where humans were judged for their deeds on Earth, and as you can imagine, not all would pass the test. If a soul didn't pass, they would be condemned to eternal damnation in the fiery lake of fire, where Ammit, the soul-eating demon of the underworld, resided. The determination to never become prey to Ammit was what propelled the people of ancient Egypt to uphold the Ma'at with their lives.

But before the test took place, souls would be draped in clean robes and given new sandals upon entering the Duat. They were then ferried to the Hall of Truth to be judged. The Hall of Truth was large and magnificent, with souls standing in long lines for trial before Osiris, the god of the underworld.

Osiris would be flanked by the god Anubis and the god Thoth. Forty-two gods (or judges) would also be present in the hall, each representing a district (or nome) in ancient Egypt. When it was a soul's turn to be judged, the soul would step forward and say the "Declaration of Innocence" before each of the forty-two judges. Here is a short example of what they would have said:

1.   "Hail Far-strider, who came forth from Heliopolis, I have done no falsehood.

2.   Hail Fire-embracer, who came forth from Kheraha, I have not robbed.

3.   Hail Nosey, who came forth from Hermopolis, I have not been rapacious.

4.   Hail Swallower of Shades, who came forth from the cavern, I have not stolen.

5.   Hail Dangerous One, who came forth from Rosetjau, I have not killed men."

These sacred confessions were a soul's testimony of having lived in line with Ma'at, and every confession had to be accepted by the gods, or else the soul was in greater danger of condemnation.

Next, their heart would be handed over for weighing by Anubis on a scale made of gold. The heart represented a person's character, personality, and values they held while on Earth. This is why the heart was typically buried with the dead in ancient Egypt.

On the other side of the golden scale would be a white ostrich feather, an aspect of Ma'at called the Feather of Truth. This test would ultimately determine if the soul was deserving of eternal life or the dreadful opposite. If the soul's heart weighed lighter than the Feather of Truth, then it meant that the soul had indeed lived a life pleasing to the gods. Their reward would be entry into the paradise of the afterlife.

If a soul's heart weighed heavier than the Feather of Truth, it meant that the soul was unjust and unfit for paradise. Their heart would be discarded in a fiery pit of fire or thrown at the soul-eating demon, Ammit. Once devoured, the soul would cease to exist and die a second death.

Ammit, the devourer of souls, as displayed in the British Museum.
https://commons.wikimedia.org/wiki/File:Ammit_BD.jpg

This was the worst fate any mortal could be condemned to, and as a result, surviving the Hall of Truth was more important to the people of Egypt than earthly riches, fame, or glory.

After the Hall of Truth was a lovely lake, known as the Lily Lake or the Lake of Flowers. Only one boat ferried souls across this lake to paradise, and the spirit in charge of the boat was named Hraf-haf. His assistant was named Aken. Hraf-haf was a mystical creature who had his head on backward, and he had a nasty temper. Even after passing the test in the Hall of Truth, the ride to paradise was not for free—at least not on Hraf-haf's watch. Some traditions claim that

Hraf-haf would challenge souls to a match of fishing. Losing meant forfeiting their place on his boat and being stranded. Other accounts insist that all it took to convince the foul-tempered ferryman was to be patient and kind, despite his provocative words and glares.

Hraf-haf was not the only obstacle in a soul's path to paradise. There were other perils, such as being attacked by demons who guarded the many gates leading to paradise. These gates were either fifteen or twenty-one in number, and souls had to be on guard to ward off evil spirits.

Aaru, or the Field of Reeds, was the final destination for every soul that survived the ordeals of the Lily Lake. It was located in the east, where the sun rose, and it was usually depicted as a beautiful island with endless fields that stretched breathtakingly to the horizon.

Here, souls could live as they had on Earth. They could have farmlands and harvest crops since the weather and climatic conditions in Aaru were perpetually perfect for cultivation.

Souls could eat and drink and have parties and sex. In Aaru, the social order was preserved. Pharaohs in ancient Egypt were commonly buried with many servants because those servants would assume their duties in Aaru. Possessions that a soul, king or not, needed in the afterlife would be buried with them. These would be given to them in Aaru to be used for their convenience forever.

The Duat: Home of the Gods

You may have heard of Mount Olympus in Greek mythology or Valhalla in Norse mythology. These were the homes of the gods, and so was the Duat of Egyptian mythology. In the earlier perception of Duat as a celestial home above the earth and its eventual perception as an underworld below the earth, ancient Egyptians across all eras agreed on the existence of gods in the Duat.

The first god in the Duat was the god Osiris, following a dreadful incident with his brother Set on Earth. According to ancient texts, Osiris ruled the underworld as brilliantly as he had on Earth. His brilliant knowledge of the underworld was a guiding light for other gods who resided and worked in Duat as judges, guardians, protectors, and friends of mortal souls.

While souls waited to be judged in the Hall of Truth, they were cared for by goddesses like Isis, Nephthys, Hathor, and Qebhet. These goddesses only catered to souls they had been invoked to care for during burial. Apart from Anubis's role as the Weigher of Hearts, the god was the one who stood at the gates of the Duat to usher in souls. His companion, the god Thoth, was a counselor for souls who sought wisdom in the afterlife. They would visit him in his mansion in Aaru for this. The houses of gods and goddesses in the afterlife were more magnificent than their earthly temples, and only the righteous and just would live to see them.

The sun god Ra was another frequent guest in the Duat. Every night, he would come by in his divine boat, the Atet, after an arduous fight with the Serpent of Chaos, Apophis (or Apep). He would spend the ten hours of night revitalizing the souls in the Duat with his solar energy, and at the break of dawn, he would ascend to the sky as the sun.

This was a repeat cycle that was vital to the preservation of Ma'at; it was one that should never be disrupted. Also, with Apophis (Apep) lurking in ambush for the sun god each night, the inhabitants of the underworld would look forward to being witnesses to an epic battle and Ra's victory, something that would always happen to preserve Ma'at.

PART TWO: MYTHS AND LEGENDS

Chapter 4 – Ra and Apophis

If you have ever wondered how night becomes day, imagine a certain famous god taking eternal trips through a world of dark and the dead and battling a ferocious monster to bring the sun out the next day. Such was the journey of Ra.

By now, you know of Ra, the Egyptian sun god and the sun itself. You also know his status in divinity and his prominence among the gods who laid the foundations of Egypt and the whole world as it has existed for many generations.

One of the core tenets of Egyptian mythology is the emphasis on the intervention of the gods (supernatural beings) in the affairs of humans (mortal beings). This established a complex religious system, and it has been proven to have existed during the Old Kingdom. These beliefs were derived from ancient Egyptian carvings and texts from prehistory. In them were the stories of legendary battles describing the might of the gods and how their victories preserved the earth, its elements, and all who lived on it.

One of these battles was between the sun god Ra and his archenemy, a serpentine villain called Apophis (or Apep). Snakes are creatures both dreaded and revered in Egyptian mythology. You will recall that the goddesses of the Ogdoad were portrayed as having snake heads. Even Ra is often portrayed as having a snake resting on the sun disk on his head. So, snakes did not outrightly symbolize evil.

Apophis, however, was a snake at the foot of the underworld, and he was as evil as they came. He represented chaos, darkness, and utter destruction, and he was known among both gods and men.

The name Apophis is first mentioned in documents from the Egyptian Middle Kingdom (c. 2030 BCE and 1640 BCE), which came right after the Old Kingdom.

Stories of the evil serpent's origins vary from one religious cult and location to the other, but all accounts affirm that Apophis came from Ra. Some even hold that the serpent came forth from Ra's umbilical cord, but no traditions actually refer to Apophis as an offspring of Ra. This is possibly due to Apophis's hatred of Ra and his quest to destroy the sun god by interfering with his earthly responsibilities.

What were these responsibilities, you wonder? Well, since his emergence as the solar god, Ra was chiefly responsible for separating day from night. His daily routine was to travel in the sky in his solar barque (or a chariot of some sort), which was the sun itself. Imagine the sun as a bright flaming barque floating in the clouds and spreading its radiance everywhere it passes; that would be the god Ra at work.

When evening came, Ra would make his slow descent into the underworld on the western horizon; this is why the sun always sets in the west. After spending the night in the underworld, Ra's little ship would rise to the skies again in the east.

Ra never traveled alone. With him on his floating vessel were soldiers (or defenders), such as the god Set (before he turned evil) and the Eye of Ra. They helped protect the sun god.

Midway in their descent to the underworld, Ra and his entourage would be beset by Apophis. Usually, Apophis would lurk around a mountain in the west known as Bakhu at sunset or somewhere in the underworld before the crack of dawn. Ra could never predict where the serpent was waiting to attack, which is why one of Apophis's aliases is the "Encircler of the World." Apophis was a prisoner who could never live on Earth or even in the underworld. He would block the sun god's path to the underworld, and he would not be removed until he was defeated. A few stories suggest that Apophis was bitter since the sun god had overthrown him as the god of gods, but many agree that the serpent was evil from the onset.

Thus, a battle would ensue every night between the sun god and Apophis. Sometimes, the sun god fought alone, and other times, he would have some help from members of his entourage, notably the god Set and Bastet, the fierce goddess of protection. She would take the form of a celestial cat and fight Apophis since cats and snakes were known to be natural enemies.

It should be emphasized that Apophis was a formidable opponent. He was not a mortal creature, so he was incredibly tough to kill, even for a god. He could be repelled, imprisoned, weakened, or dismembered at best. Apophis could eat anything and yet not kill it. Instead, what he ate would be lost forever in a dark abyss, never to taste death or the afterlife. He could prey on the living or dead, gods or mortals. In some accounts, he commanded an army of demons in his likeness. Apophis's eyes held the power of hypnosis, another weapon he wielded in warfare. Ra would sometimes be hypnotized by Apophis, but the gods and goddesses in his company would move swiftly to his rescue.

To mark the start of every battle, Apophis would let out an ear-splitting roar and slither violently toward the sun god. His charge was what caused earthquakes. Every time Set speared Apophis, pinning him to the ground, Apophis would wriggle in brutal rage and roar in pain, causing thunderstorms on the earth.

However, despite Apophis's dreadful outlook, it was never heard of for Ra to lose a battle to the snake. A few times, the sun god would be swallowed by Apophis; this was believed to be the cause of solar eclipses. But in the end, Ra would win the battle. He would tear his way out of the beast's belly and vanquish Apophis, usually with the help of his army of gods and goddesses.

The sun god could not lose to Apophis because that would mark the end of the sun god. If there was no sun god, there would be no sun. And without the sun, there would be no daytime. Without daytime, Earth and mankind would be doomed to perpetual darkness.

Knowing how important Ra's victory was to their existence, mortals would not leave the nightly war between darkness and light to chance.

The Banishment of Apophis

"Get thee back, Apep, thou enemy of Ra, thou winding serpent in the form of an intestine, without arms [and] without legs. Thy body cannot stand upright so that thou mayest have therein being, long is thy tail in front of thy den, thou enemy; retreat before Ra. Thy head shall be cut off, and the slaughter of thee shall be carried out."

-Excerpt from an ancient hieroglyphic spell translated by Sir Wallis Budge

Every year in Egypt, a momentous occasion brought all the worshipers and priests of Ra together in temples throughout the land. The occasion would ensure the victory of the sun god against his vengeful opponent, Apophis, and preserve the order of the world (also known as Ma'at).

Of all the supernatural beings in Egyptian mythology, only Apophis was actively worshiped against. There was no motive for his evil nature, and he had no good side to him. He hated mortals and only sought their annihilation, so rituals and rites had to be adhered to in order to keep Apophis and his wickedness at bay.

The most prominent of these rites was the Banishment of Apophis, also known as the Banishment of Apep or the Banishment of Chaos. This ritual was held in all the provinces of ancient Egypt, as they were all united against a common enemy. The success of this ritual would guarantee the sun god's victory for the next year.

The Banishment of Apophis would begin with the crafting of an effigy or statue representing the serpent. This effigy would be made to bear all the curses and evil of the land and then burned to ashes, which symbolizes the destruction of Apophis. In other temples, images of Apophis would be illustrated on papyruses. They would then be cursed and burned.

These rituals were led by priests, who were guided by a special book titled the "Book of Apophis." The book outlined instructions on other ways to defy Apophis, apart from burning his image. These included spitting on Apophis, trampling on him with the left foot, putting chains on Apophis, and stabbing him with lances or knives. These rites expressed the people's disdain for the evil serpent, and they were believed to give strength to their champion, the sun god, in battle.

Apophis was also an eater of the dead. The Egyptians feared their dead might become prey to the serpent's monstrous appetites, so they buried spells and incantations to repel Apophis with their dead. This would protect their souls in the afterlife from destruction.

The legend of Ra and Apophis had a tremendous influence on the religious affairs of ancient Egypt. It gave the people a sense of duty to preserve their existence by keeping evil under subjugation. Every time the sun rose the next day, they were assured that the sun god Ra had won another victory.

Chapter 5 – The Osiris Myth

Pyramids were all the rage in the Old and Middle Kingdoms. Just by looking at pictures of them, you wonder how much time, money, and effort it took to build something so majestic. The answer is a lot. Such resources would not be expended by people who were passive or agnostic about the afterlife.

Egyptians who were not kings were also uniquely buried for a smooth passage to the afterlife. The corpses of nobles were typically mummified: embalmed and wrapped in bandages made from linen, then buried facing the east (where the sun rose). This way, their spirits would rise up and join the sun god on his eternal journey to and from the underworld. Commoners who could not afford the process of mummification left the bodies of their deceased out in the desert sun for more than two months as a method of embalmment. Even though pyramid-building was seen as old-fashioned in the New Kingdom, the Egyptian belief in life after death remained, as did the funeral rites to ensure the deceased's passage.

What was the foundation of this unwavering Egyptian faith, you wonder? It was a myth. The most popular myth in Egyptian mythology at that. It was based on a very intriguing family feud. This chapter puts the spotlight on the myth of Osiris, the god-king who transitioned gloriously to the afterlife despite the rather sordid circumstances.

<u>Family Feud</u>

In the creation story of Heliopolis, the sun god Ra's grandchildren, Geb and Nut, had four to five children before they were forced to separate by their father, Shu, who did not quite approve of their union.

Now, this story begins at a time when Egypt was ruled by Osiris, the first son of Geb and Nut. Our protagonist's earthly form was a handsome bearded young man draped in royal raiment and a feathered headdress (called an Atef) set upon his jet-black hair. His charm and charisma were amplified by his rare wisdom, which he used to rule Egypt.

An image of Osiris.
Credit: Unknown author, CC0, via Wikimedia Commons;
https://commons.wikimedia.org/wiki/File:The_Sacred_Books_and_Early_Literature_of_the_East,_vo
l._2,_pg._64-65,_Osiris.jpg

The exact time that Osiris was the ruler of Egypt is unknown, which is why historical texts commonly refer to him as a "pre-dynastic" or "primeval" king. At the very least, it can be assumed that Osiris inherited the throne from his father Geb, who was the god of the earth.

Osiris's reign was marked by significant reforms in the lives of the people. First, he outlawed cannibalism in Egypt. In place of such barbarism, Osiris guided his people to look to alternatives like growing their own food on arable land. He blessed all who raised bountiful harvests for their sustenance. This earned Osiris the divine title as the god of fertility, agriculture, and vegetation.

Another highlight of Osiris's reign appears in Plutarch's famous work *Moralia*. This was the improvement of Egypt's artistic culture. Music and dance flourished in Egypt under Osiris's watchful eye, and one day, he embarked on a worldwide voyage to spread this newfound civilization. The god-king visited many lands in Europe and the Near East, bringing the world into a new era of arts and culture. Before leaving home, Osiris entrusted the rulership of Egypt to his wife, who was also his sister, Isis.

Queen Isis adored her husband and held the fort in his absence, despite her secret pains of not having borne him an heir. She had watched her husband administer a kingdom, instilling its people with the virtues of truth, fairness, and justice to the people. She resolved to preserve the standards by being an amiable ruler.

When she received the king's mandate to rule in his stead until he returned, little did she know that a deathly scheme was in the works. This sinister plot was being championed by her other brother, Set.

In the Egyptian corpus, you will find divergent versions of Set's motive for harming a good king. The Greek historian Plutarch suggests that Set had long harbored jealous and envious feelings toward his brother's fortune and peaceful reign over Egypt. He coveted the throne and everything his older brother had. This speaks to a motive that is mostly, if not wholly, influenced by Set's bad nature. After all, he was the god of violent chaos and war. He is represented as a red-haired creature with physical resemblances to multiple animals, including hyenas, jackals, pigs, and foxes.

Other accounts, notably from the Pyramid Texts, infer that Set's hatred toward his brother may have had deeper roots. Some tales say that Osiris slept with Set's wife (and sister), Nephthys, with their illicit affair resulting in the birth of Anubis. In the god-king's defense, Nephthys had deceived him by taking on the form of Osiris's wife, Isis, and he had slept with her thinking it was truly his wife.

Plutarch tells us that Set would not be appeased. Enraged at his brother, Set swore that he would kill Osiris. Set quickly rallied a small group of conspirators. King Osiris was loved by too many people for Set to easily find accomplices, so he bribed a few dishonorable men to his side or manipulated them with words. While the god-king was away on his trip, Set and his men hatched a dark plan.

Soon enough, Set announced he would hold a grand banquet at his place, possibly to celebrate his brother's return from his successful tour of the world. The day came, and it saw the attendance of numerous guests, including King Osiris himself. There was food, wine, and a rather peculiar party favor: a coffin (sometimes written as a chest) fashioned from the highest quality materials in all the land.

Such a coffin would no doubt allow for a most comfortable journey to the afterlife, and nearly every guest in the banquet hall coveted it. Their desire to own the coffin surged when Set announced that the coffin was a prize to be won.

The challenge was simple. One had to step into the coffin and lay inside it. Whoever fit into the coffin perfectly could have it. Set's guests leaped out of their seats for a chance to win it. A good number of them tried to get in the coffin, but none could fit. Guest after guest attempted, and guest after guest failed. This was because the dimensions of the coffin could never fit anyone else in Egypt, save for one: King Osiris himself.

Excited to participate in the game, the king stepped into the coffin and lay inside it. It was a match so perfect that the guests wondered if it was made specifically for the king. In the time it took for them to explore their curiosities, Set swung into action, slamming the coffin shut and coating it with lead.

The reality of Set's evil plan unfolded like a scroll before the people. The coffin had indeed been made for the king. It was all a fatal trap.

Set ordered the coffin be dumped into the depths of the Nile River, sentencing his brother to a most agonizing death. The coffin submerged into the Nile and vanished from sight. All of Egypt was forced to follow a new king.

<u>Redemption and Revenge</u>

Poor Isis learned of the tragedy that had befallen her husband at the hands of Set. Consumed with sorrow, she escaped from the palace and took to searching every inch of the Nile River for the god-king's body. If she could find him, she could heal him with her magical powers, or she could give him a king's funeral if it was too late. The Nile River was a vast expanse of water to search, so the queen must have been at it for a long time. A few traditions say that she ran into Anubis during her journey. He had been cast aside by his mother, Nephthys, and hated by his father, Set, because he was Osiris's son. Queen Isis took Anubis in and raised him as her own.

Meanwhile, Egypt had erupted in anarchy under Set's reign. All of King Osiris's good work had nearly come undone, and the people suffered as a result. They no longer lived peaceful and prosperous lives.

The queen's resilience paid off one auspicious day. Isis heard the news that the coffin had drifted across the Nile to a small city in

Phoenicia called Byblos. As it turned out, Osiris's coffin had washed ashore in Byblos. A tamarisk tree grew around it, trapping the coffin in its trunk. King Osiris's residual powers made this deciduous tree flourish season after season while having a distinct fragrance. Some accounts state that the tree could even glow.

It occurred to King Malcander of Byblos and his wife, Queen Astarte (or Ishtar), that it was no ordinary tamarisk tree. The king ordered that the tree be cut down, and he had an ornamental pillar made out of it. This pillar stood in his palace to the envy of all who laid eyes upon it.

The palace of Byblos had many court ladies who tended to the royal family with their skills in child-nursing, grooming, and cloth and perfume making. One day, a frail old woman arrived at the palace gates and pleaded to have an audience with the queen.

Unknown to the people of Byblos, they had just received the goddess Isis, and she was on an important rescue mission. As part of the plan to save Osiris, Isis (in disguise) petitioned Queen Astarte for a job in the palace. If she planned to stay in Byblos, she needed the job to stay near her trapped husband.

The queen of Byblos graciously accepted Isis into her service and entrusted Isis with the care of her son. In gratitude, Isis resolved to immortalize the young prince. It was a magic ritual process that involved bathing the baby in fire to burn away his mortality. A disguised Isis began the ritual that night, but she was interrupted by the boy's mother.

Astarte must have been horrified to find her son's nurse bathing him with fire. She demanded an explanation. It was at that moment that Isis revealed her true identity. The queen of Byblos was entranced to discover that she housed a goddess under her roof. She worshiped Isis, who then revealed her true intent. Without hesitation, the king and queen of Byblos granted Isis's request, and the coffin was removed from inside the pillar.

By then, Osiris was as good as dead, but his wife would not give up. She returned to Egypt and healed him. Many accounts agree that Horus the Younger, the son of Isis and Osiris, was born around this time.

Set, who was ruling Egypt, heard the news of his brother's survival, and he was not pleased. His wife Nephthys had begun to regret her role in the war between her brothers, as well as her abandonment of Anubis.

Set ordered the arrest and detainment of Isis, and for his brother Osiris, he ordered a second death. Plutarch argues that this happened as soon as Isis stepped foot on Egyptian soil with her convalescing husband.

Isis escaped detainment with Anubis's help, but Osiris was not so lucky. Set took advantage of his weakness and violently murdered him. Afterward, Set dismembered Osiris's corpse into fourteen pieces and dispersed them, making sure each piece was far apart from another. Such aggression was Set's twisted way of ensuring that Osiris would not make it back alive again.

Isis mourned Osiris's inhumane demise and set out with her sister, Nephthys, and Horus to find and reassemble Osiris's mutilated body parts. Their quest was a success, at least for the most part. The sisters were able to recover all of Osiris's body parts except his penis. Set had discarded it in the depths of the Nile River, and fish had eaten it. Some stories say that Isis fashioned him a new one made out of wood, while others say she used magic.

With Isis's powers, Osiris came back to life, but he was no longer complete. This made him unfit to reclaim his throne. Instead, he transitioned to the underworld, where he became its god and the judge of the dead.

That was hardly the end of Isis's troubles. Set was still on the rampage, searching high and low for her son Horus. Set sought to take his life just as he had taken his father's.

Isis fled to the marshlands of Egypt with her son, and there, she raised him. Horus grew from boy to man, sharpening his sword of revenge. He learned all about spells and the art of warfare. His archenemy was the god of war himself, and his mother raised him not to be a pushover.

Horus grew to become a mighty warrior and Set's arch-nemesis. Egypt was on the verge of desolation under his cruel rule, and the impoverished people of Egypt found a beacon of hope in Horus. They offered him their support and followed in vast numbers when he led the charge against the tyrant Set.

Set was removed from the throne of Egypt; some say he was killed, while others believe he was exiled into the Red Sea. It is unknown if he reached a new shore or if he continues to drift upon the waves. Most importantly, this tale ends in a resounding victory for the son of Osiris, whose reign would be a soothing balm to a wounded Egypt.

Chapter 6 – Time and the End of Times

Discovering the measurement of time and its passage was a great feat for many ancient civilizations, the ancient Egyptians included.

As you can imagine, there were no wall clocks, wristwatches, or grandfather clocks in the Old and Middle Kingdoms. Still, people needed to keep track of time to figure out how best to apply it to daily living. Only time could separate a day from another day, a week from another week, and a year from another year.

The sun god Ra and his company made trips to and from the underworld every day on his chariot or boat, and the ancient Egyptians got to work themselves to seek the answers of time and space. In the chronology of discoveries, it is agreeable that ancient Egyptians had figured out the "End of Times" first.

The End of Times

The "End of Times" is used to describe the final stage of cosmology: the end of the world as we know it. It refers to an event where the world, humans, and possibly the gods are no longer in existence. In ancient Egypt, it was a time when the world went back to being a void and was supplanted by what had existed in the first place: Nun.

There are two perspectives to the ancient Egyptian belief in the "End of Times." The first perspective was prevalent when the gods ruled the earth as kings. The second perspective slightly reshaped the Egyptian belief system from the Old Kingdom to after the New Kingdom, when Christianity came to Egypt.

The First Perspective: Gods and Men

Compared to other ancient civilizations, such as Mesopotamia and Greece, the ancient Egyptian belief system initially perceived the end of the world as a mistake to be avoided rather than an eventuality.

How you wonder?

Take Greece and Mesopotamia, for instance. Both civilizations believed there would be a flood, similar to the biblical story about Noah, where a flood destroyed the earth. In Mesopotamian mythology, when the flood came, the humans would have to build arks—just like Noah in the Bible did—to save themselves. In the Greek flood myth, only a man named Deucalion and his wife survived the flood by hiding out in a chest.

These flood myths were told in Greece and Mesopotamia as inevitable events and some sort of inescapable punishment for mankind. The nature of the ancient Egyptian perspective on the End of the World (or the apocalypse) was not inevitable.

You are familiar with the sun god's daily routine and how important it is to the preservation of Ma'at. You should also recall that the Egyptians of old played a big role in giving their gods the strength to perform their divine tasks through prayers and worship. Their greatest fear was that if they faltered, the gods could become weak and falter. The eventuality of this would be a disruption in the natural order, but that would be only the tip of a disastrous iceberg.

If gods like Ra ever lost their strength and had no worshipers to invigorate them, they could die.

The death of the gods would spell the end of the world, and the murder of the god-king Osiris by his brother Set was a close call. Chaos befell Egypt after Osiris's death, and were it not for the resilience of Queen Isis and the victory of Horus the Younger, the destruction of Ma'at would have been complete. Ma'at had also been shaken to its core when Shu, the son of Ra, had left his throne on Earth and ascended to the sky. A violent storm ravaged the world for nine days, and no god or man could enjoy a moment of clarity until Geb was enthroned.

So, the preservation of Ma'at in the ancient Egyptian belief system was a joint effort by the gods and the humans who worshiped them. As long as each one played their part, the "End of Times" would remain an avoidable consequence.

From another viewpoint, rather than large-scale destruction and the harvesting of souls, the Egyptians perceived the predestined "End of Times" as strictly individualistic. No human could escape death, and after someone died, there was an afterlife where they would spend eternity.

In the Pyramid Texts and other ancient documents, the end of the world was evoked in a peculiar manner. It was seen as a threat to the gods. This is incredibly ironic, considering that ancient Egyptians revered their gods. However, Egyptians were known to threaten the gods with mayhem if their prayers were not answered.

"O Lord of the horizon, make ready a place for me. For if you fail to make ready a place for me, I will lay a curse on my father Geb, and the earth will speak no more, Geb will be unable to protect himself, and whoever I find in my way, I will devour him piecemeal."

Many variants of these kinds of threats can be found in the Coffin Texts (more information on them can be found in Chapter 19), spell books, and medical journals from the Old Kingdom.

Did these threats ever move the gods to action? Shockingly, they did. The gods wanted Ma'at to be sustained just as much as the mortals. They considered such "worship threats" to be expressions of fervent prayers, and they responded swiftly to all who evoked them. This remains a fascinating aspect of ancient Egyptians' worship of the gods.

The Second Perspective: Men

This saga is set in Early Dynastic Egypt.

The gods no longer ruled men, at least not directly. They were still involved in the affairs of nature and order. Humans still worshiped the gods and looked up to the pharaoh as a guiding light and the messenger of the gods.

The first pharaoh of a united Egypt was Menes (or Narmer, according to some). He established the First Dynasty sometime in the 3000s BCE in ancient Egypt. He is best known for uniting Upper and Lower Egypt under a single ruler. This made Menes and the other pharaohs after him very powerful.

This became problematic in the long run, though. With the rule of the pharaohs over a united Egypt came an influx of apocalyptic prophecies, each describing a very dramatic "End of Times." These prophecies have been criticized as propaganda-driven, as they typically proffered the reign of a certain pharaoh as the only way to avert the coming danger. However, these stories of a looming apocalypse shifted ancient Egypt's belief system from the god-centric perspective it once held.

First, there was the Prophecy of Neferti.

Sometime in the mid-2000s BCE, the Fourth Dynasty of ancient Egypt was established by the reigning pharaoh, Snefru. King Snefru's kingdom was vast and prosperous, extending to the lands of Libya and Nubia (Sudan). He also commanded a massive labor force and was wealthy in land and cattle.

One day, Pharaoh Snefru was in high spirits and sought to be entertained by an excellent lyrical poet or sage. The men in the king's court recommended a man named Neferti as being best suited for the job.

The king trusted his courtiers and had Neferti brought before him immediately. After paying homage to the pharaoh, Neferti presented the king with two kinds of stories: stories of the past and stories of the future.

It seemed as if Neferti was living up to his reputation. Since Snefru was the pharaoh of Egypt, there was nothing about the past he did not know. He was a revered custodian of knowledge of the gods and the long history of Egypt. But he did not know of the future.

Without hesitation, King Snefru chose to hear stories of the future. Neferti's story, as the king was about to find out, was a prophecy of doom.

"I show you the land in turmoil; what should not be has come to pass. Men will seize weapons of warfare, the land will live in uproar. Men will make arrows of copper, will crave blood for bread, will laugh aloud at distress. None will weep over death, none will wake fasting for death...

Ra will withdraw from mankind: though he will rise at his hour, one will not know when noon has come; no one will discern his shadow, no face will be dazzled by seeing [him], no eyes will moisten with water. He will be in the sky like the moon, his nightly course unchanged, his rays on the face as before."

The first part of Neferti's prophecy described political unrest, civil war, and social anarchy; this is not quite enough to be apocalyptic. It also limited the disaster to Egypt as a nation. However, the second part of the prophecy where Ra is mentioned transformed Neferti's speech from a mere prediction to a prophecy of cosmological bedlam.

King Snefru and his courtiers must have been horrified to hear of such things as the Nile drying up or Ra turning his back on mankind. These events symbolized an age of overwhelming evil and the termination of Ma'at, but there was a resolution: "Then a king will come from the South, Ameny by name...Then Order will return to its seat, while Chaos is driven away."

As it would turn out, this king from the south was Amenemhat I, who would rule Egypt eight dynasties later. Glorifying a pharaoh as the bringer of peace to a disrupted land—and inadvertently the whole world—further established the supremacy of the Egyptian monarchy.

The gods were no longer the sole centerpiece of the people's belief in the "End of Times." Their salvation was now in the hands of a mortal man. Neferti's apocalyptic message surfaced at a time when the kings of Egypt had better positioned themselves as the messiahs of the people. As important intermediaries between the gods and the people, the pharaohs were worshiped and offered the same sacrifices as the gods.

Despite being set hundreds of years earlier, the recovered document containing the Prophecy of Neferti was written around the Twelfth Dynasty, during the reign of the king that was prophesied about. Convenient, don't you think?

This has left historians skeptical about the authenticity of the prophecy. It was possibly a ruse to justify Amenemhat's alleged usurpation of the Egyptian throne from King Mentuhotep IV, whom he had served as a vizier.

The Book of Asclepius: Back to Divinity

In the 1st to 3rd centuries CE, ancient Egypt underwent what some might consider a Roman invasion. During this period, ancient Egypt became a Roman province whose political and religious mythical beliefs were fused with Graeco-Roman mythology. This fusion is known as syncretism.

For example, the Greek god Zeus was fused with the Egyptian god Amun, becoming Zeus-Ammon. Ra was the equivalent of Apollo, Aphrodite was the equivalent of Queen Isis, and the Greek god Hermes was the equivalent of the Egyptian god Thoth.

The syncretism of Hermes and Thoth created a mythical author named Hermes Trismegistus, and in the 4th century CE, a sacred apocalyptic text written by this legendary figure was found in Egypt. It was part of a large document called the *Corpus Hermeticum*, and the prophecy inside it was titled the "Book of Asclepius."

This prophecy had a chilling melancholic tone:

"A time will come when it will be seen that in vain the Egyptians served the deity with piety and assiduous service, and all their holy worship will be found fruitless and to no profit. For the deity will retire from earth to heaven, and Egypt will be forsaken; and the land which was the home of religion will be left desolate, bereft of the presence of its gods. Foreigners will fill this country, and not only will the observances be neglected, but even more terrible, it will be made compulsory by so-called laws, under pain of prescribed punishments, to abstain from all religious practices, from any act of piety towards the gods. This most holy land, country of sanctuaries and temples, will be covered with sepulchers and corpses."

This apocalypse, dreadful as it is, ends with a message of hope and rebirth orchestrated by the gods. This prophecy was given by the god Thoth to Asclepius, a demi-god in Graeco-Roman mythology, and it was documented by Hermes Trismegistus. It was a three-pronged message of predestination, and unlike the Prophecy of Neferti, it resonated with the reality of the times. Egypt was under Roman subjugation after a war-torn era, and according to the prophecy, more turbulence lay ahead in order for the world to be cleansed. Most significant of all, the salvation of the world was not in the hands of any man; rather, it was in the hands of a divine being who could neither be bribed nor controlled.

There remains debate as to whether Hermes Trismegistus, the acclaimed author of this apocalyptic prophecy, actually existed. Yet he was an influential figure in Graeco-Roman and Egyptian mythology as a patron of writing.

The Telling of Time

A long time ago, there were no alarm clocks and fashionable wristwatches to tell the time by. Such technologies were not to be discovered until thousands of years later. Still, people had to figure out what time of the day it was or what season was best to do this or that in.

Ancient Egypt had one of the richest civilizations of its time; there is no doubt about that. And Egyptians are credited with some of the earliest innovations of telling the time. This was possible because they believed in the sun god's journey of separating day from night. From as early as 3500 BCE, Egyptians had developed a unique lunar calendar that had thirty days in twelve months: a total of 360 days.

Rather than summer, spring, winter, or autumn, ancient Egypt's seasons were named Akhet, Peret, and Shemu.

Akhet: The Flooding of the Nile

Akhet was also known as the "Season of the Inundation" or the "Season of the Flood." Believed to be the first season in the year, Akhet had four months: *Thout*, named after the ancient Egyptian god of wisdom and science; *Paopi*, named after a famous festival celebrated that month in honor of Ra; *Hathor*, named after the ancient Egyptian goddess of the sky; and *Koiak*, named after a sacred bull in ancient Egypt.

The Akhet season marked the momentous flooding of the Nile River. Since the Nile River was the main source of Egypt's water supply, every time the waters overflowed, the lands would regain their fertility. As you are bound to notice, the Nile River was the centerpiece of the ancient Egyptian calendar in its entirety. The division of time into days, months, and years was an innovation resulting from a close observation of the Nile's patterns. Akhet brought bountiful water to the Nile, more so than any other time of the year, and it marked the start of a new agricultural season.

Akhet also marked colorful religious festivities in honor of the sun god Ra and the goddess Hathor. During the New Kingdom, rituals and festivals in honor of Osiris, Isis, and Nephthys became popular in the month of *Koiak*.

The equivalent of the Akhet season in modern-day calendars falls between September and January.

Peret: The Planting Season

After four months of enriching the soils of Egypt, the Nile River would pull back, leaving the land ripe for planting. Ancient Egyptians called this season Peret or the "Season of Emergence." The word "emergence" refers to the lands along the Nile River, which reemerged after being flooded with water during the Akhet season.

Peret also had four months (approximately between January and May), which gave farmers ample time to plow their lands and plant their seeds. The first month in Peret (or the fifth month in the year) was *Tobi*, named after one of the many forms of the god Ra. Next was *Meshir*, named after the ancient Egyptian god of the wind. *Paremhat* came next, and it was named after a pharaoh who reigned in the 1500s BCE. And the last month of the season, *Pharmouthi* or *Paremoude*, was named in deference to the ancient Egyptian goddess of nourishment and the harvest, Renenutet.

Since the ancient Egyptians were busy cultivating their farmlands, it is no surprise that no elaborate festivals or rituals were celebrated during the Peret season. Instead, they would offer up prayers to

Min and Renenutet, the god and goddess of the harvest, to bless their lands and bring them a plentiful harvest in the coming season.

Shemu: A Bountiful Harvest

The harvest season was the most anticipated time of the year in ancient Egypt. The Nile River at this time was at its lowest, and the new crops sprouting from the ground were ready for reaping in the Shemu season, also known as the "Season of Harvest." There would be fresh food in Egypt, a reward for many months of labor.

The Shemu season was also the driest; it would be the equivalent of summer (May to September), with four months marking the end of the year. The first month of the season (and the ninth month of the year) was *Pashons*, a derivative of the god of the moon and son of Ra, Khonsu. After it came *Paoni*, which was named after the festival of the dead (the Valley Festival), which was celebrated during the month. The next month was *Epip*, and after it was *Mesori*, which celebrated the end of the harvest season and the New Year.

Festivities to mark the end of the year were held in honor of Ra, and the thirtieth day of *Mesori* was a special holiday in ancient Egypt. It was the last day of the year, and a series of intriguing events were planned. First, every royal artisan (sculptors, carpenters, painters, smiths, builders, and scribes who lived in the palace) could take the day off work. They joined the townspeople to perform sacred rites. Every temple in Egypt was fortified with spells and torches to ward off evil while the people celebrated. If there were any new pharaohs to be crowned, this was typically the season to do it, and every sitting pharaoh would receive goodwill gifts from his retainers.

As the streets of Egypt lit up in anticipation of the New Year, the people would exchange gifts in good faith. After having harvested and stored enough food in the Shemu season, the people of ancient Egypt would not need to worry about their survival during the coming Akhet season when the Nile would flood again.

Sundials, Shadow Clocks, and Merkhets

The most important highlight in all of the ancient Egyptian seasons was the sun god's preeminence. Every season had a month named after him or one of his forms. The sun, like the Nile River, was a marker of times and seasons. The ancient Egyptians were ahead of their time; they created the first known solar calendar. They discovered the importance of the sun and its cyclical pattern and applied it in the invention of the solar calendar.

More remarkably, the ancient Egyptians were able to use the sun to tell the hours of the day with one of their inventions. The earliest time-telling device was the obelisk, a stone-carved monument with a pointed top and four corners. Obelisks were strategically erected, and their height dimensions were specific enough so they could reflect the motion of the sun. The shadow cast by the sun against a side of the obelisk represented morning or noon.

While obelisks were of tremendous use to the people who lived in Egypt over five thousand years ago, there was a small challenge—obelisks were not mobile. They were not moveable, which meant that people would have to walk miles to the nearest obelisk to be able to tell the time.

It simply would not do.

So, the Egyptians got creative again. The ideal invention had to be portable so that people would be able to tell the time wherever they went. One day, around 1500 BCE, the shadow-casting time-telling technology got a massive upgrade. Someone invented the sundial.

The Egyptian sundial.

The sundial was an intriguing artifact consisting of a flat plate called the dial and something called a gnomon on it. The gnomon was triangle-shaped and protruded out of the dial. It served a similar purpose to hands on a clock by tracing the sun's every move across the sky. Each move would cast a shadow on the dial, which would progress slowly around the plate. This allowed people to tell the hours of the day, but what happened when the sun went down?

Merkhets were used. The merkhet read the journey of stars at night, and it was typically made of wood or bone. Ancient Egyptians used this to track the movement of ten stars across the meridian. Each star represented an hour of the night, totaling ten hours for the night and an hour for the sunrise. Daytime had twelve hours and one hour for sunset, bringing the total to twenty-four hours.

Chapter 7 – The Golden Lotus

Another enthralling myth that comes to us from ancient Egypt is that of the Golden Lotus.

Nearly all of the tombs and temples discovered in ancient Egypt had carvings and representations of the lotus flower; in fact, the lotus is regarded as Egypt's national flower today.

The lotus symbolized healing, creation, and spiritual rebirth. This was inspired by how lotuses bloomed in the sunlight and closed their petals to submerge under the water at night. The next morning, the lotuses would reemerge on the water's surface, opening up their petals to herald the sun (or be "reborn"). Lotuses could only be found in ponds and lakes, and they looked as beautiful as they smelled.

In Egypt, you would find blue lotuses adorning the length of the River Nile, and they were famed across the land for their beauty and rejuvenation.

According to the creation myth in Memphis, the god Nefertum emerged as a lotus flower when the world was created by his father, Ptah. Nefertum is depicted as a beautiful young man with a lotus flower on his head, and he was worshiped as the Protector of the Two Lands (Upper and Lower Egypt).

At ancient Egyptian funerals, oil extracted from the lotus flowers was used as an ingredient to mummify the deceased and neutralize the stench of decay. In Egyptian art, there are many depictions of the gods and goddesses holding lotuses to the noses of pharaohs and queens of Egypt, symbolizing their rebirth into the afterlife.

Knowing the significance of these beautiful flowers, the myth of the Golden Lotus can be better appreciated. This story is set during the reign of Snefru (also spelled as Sneferu, the same king who received the Prophecy of Neferti). Snefru is also famed for his strides in ancient Egyptian architecture. This was a legacy continued by his son, Khufu, who built the Great Pyramid of Giza, one of the Seven Wonders of the Ancient World.

The Egyptian myth of the Golden Lotus also originates from the ancient city of Memphis, and it begins with the king feeling rather bored one day. All was well during his reign. There were no civil wars or foreign aggression. The king strolled through his majestic palace, yearning for some sort of entertainment. There were no movies or cinemas in ancient Egypt, but there was music, dancing, and magic.

King Snefru thought of his chief magician, a formidable man named Djadjaemankh. If he invited Djadjaemankh to his palace, the man could perform magic tricks that would lift his spirits. Immediately, he ordered the chief magician to be brought before him.

Djadjaemankh was summoned from his residence, the House of Wisdom. Upon appearing before the king, the chief magician worshiped Snefru and asked how he could be of service. The king expressed his desire to be entertained by a private magic show since all other forms of entertainment had become a bore.

Djadjaemankh, however, had something more outlandish in mind. Instead of a magic show in the palace, he requested the king to take a boat ride on the Nile River with the promise of something wondrous.

The pharaoh saw nothing entertaining about a boat ride—he had been on tons of them with all that time on his hands. Djadjaemankh then introduced a fresh dynamic. Instead of the regular boat rowers, the king was to take twenty beautiful virgins with him as rowers for the trip. These women needed to have long, flowing hair.

This tickled King Snefru's fascination, and he handed over the charge of preparing for the boat ride to Djadjaemankh. The magician ensured that only the most beautiful women were selected. Their oars were fashioned from the finest ebony and coated with gold.

King Snefru's best royal boat was rowed out to the Nile River, and the women, who were dressed in gold-threaded raiment, took their positions to start the journey. From his royal on-boat pavilion, the king was delighted at the view of the sparkling Nile and the beautiful women he was surrounded by. All the women wore ornaments, such as jewelry and hairpins made of pure gold—gifts from the king himself.

As the magnificent royal boat continued along the seemingly endless river, the lead rower on one side of the boat accidentally knocked off the golden lotus that held her hair in place. The golden lotus slipped into the river and was submerged in no time.

Distraught, the rower stopped her rowing, suspending the pharaoh's leisure trip. King Snefru inquired into the disturbance, and the woman narrated her plight to him. She had lost a valuable gift and sought to retrieve it.

The pharaoh, in his magnanimity, entreated the woman to be calm and continue the journey. He also promised that he would replace the lost golden lotus, but the woman refused. She wanted her old lotus back, and she would not go on without it.

Only one man could bring back a submerged lotus, and it was the man who had suggested the trip in the first place. The pharaoh ordered the chief magician to be brought before him on the boat and relayed his dilemma to him:

"Zazamankh [Djadjaemankh], my friend and brother, I have done as you advised. My royal heart is refreshed and my eyes are delighted at the sight of these lovely rowers bending to their task. As we pass up and down on the waters of the lake, and they sing to me, while on the shore I see the trees and the flowers and the birds, I seem to be sailing into the golden days either those of old when Re ruled on earth, or those to come when the good god Osiris shall return from the Duat.

But now a golden lotus has fallen from the hair of one of these maidens fallen to the bottom of the lake. And she has ceased to sing and the rowers on her side cannot keep time with their oars. And she is not to be comforted with promises of other gifts, but weeps for her golden lotus. Zazamankh, I wish to give back the golden lotus to the little one here, and see the joy return to her eyes."

This was Djadjaemankh's cue to perform a most glorious deed. He assured the king and everyone on the boat that the lotus would be retrieved. The magician moved to the back of the boat and faced the vast waters, holding his magic wand. After a recital of spells and incantations, Djadjaemankh stretched out his wand over the water, and a rushing sound shook the currents.

Slowly, the waters gave way "as if a piece had been cut out of it with a great sword." The lake had parted into two halves, and the cut-out part was mounted on each side to make high cliffs of water.

No one on the boat could believe their eyes.

With Djadjaemankh leading the way, the royal boat dived into the open depths of the lake and drifted to the bottom, where it was as dry as land. It did not take too long to spot the golden lotus, and the woman who had lost it quickly retrieved it, overjoyed.

Djadjaemankh levitated the king's boat to the surface and returned the cut-out piece of the lake back to its place, closing up the waters. The pharaoh was beyond impressed by such a show of the supernatural. He applauded Djadjaemankh in the noblest words he had ever spoken to a retainer: "Zazamankh [Djadjaemankh], my brother, you are the greatest and wisest of magicians! You have shown me wonders and delights this day, and your reward shall be all that you desire, and a place next to my own in Egypt."

The king had had enough entertainment to last him the day—and possibly a lifetime—so the royal boat sailed for the palace with songs of the wondrous deeds of Djadjaemankh. The story of the golden lotus was on the lips of all who had witnessed it.

A prominent theme of this famous Egyptian myth is restoration and healing. The golden lotus in this story symbolizes everything valuable: health, wealth, and life itself. The myth also hinges on hope and second chances, possibly alluding to the afterlife. The pharaoh's kindness and that of Djadjaemankh illustrate the kindness of the gods to every believer who earnestly requests their help.

The Golden Lotus myth also bears a resemblance to the biblical story of Moses parting the Red Sea during the exodus of the Hebrews from Egypt. Both stories are parallels, but they share the common theme of faith in the supernatural and the reward of divine intervention.

Chapter 8 – The Greek Princess

The precedents of the myth of the Greek princess take us far beyond the shores of ancient Egypt to a foreign land in Greece called Sparta. It was one of the most powerful Greek nations in antiquity, and Spartan King Tyndareus and his wife Leda had a beautiful daughter named Helen.

In Greek mythology, Helen was the daughter of Zeus (equal to the Egyptian sun god Ra), and her beauty was unrivaled. Helen's beauty had attracted a good number of eligible bachelors to King Tyndareus's palace, putting him in a dilemma of who to choose. Eventually, Helen's groom was chosen from among the suitors, and Helen of Sparta was married.

Our story focuses on ancient Egypt during the chaotic reign of Pharaoh Seti II, son of Merneptah and grandson of the most powerful pharaoh of the New Kingdom, Ramesses II.

Pharaoh Seti II was engulfed in the plots to enthrone his half-brother Amenmesse as king over the major cities in Upper Egypt. Egypt had been united almost two thousand years earlier by King Menes, so there was no reason for two kings to rule the land—unless it was mutiny.

A Party of Strangers

As the king repelled the forces that threatened a partition of his kingdom, a strange boat docked on the eastern shores of the Nile River, Canopus. The boat had just weathered a violent storm from the north and had been driven off its course.

The men on the boat had finally found refuge on Egyptian soil after many days at sea, and on the horizon stood the great temple of Hershef, god of the riverbanks. Hershef was also the god who protected strangers and freed slaves from captivity if they bowed to him.

The Egyptian warden in charge of the shores of Canopus was a man named Thonis, and when he learned that strangers had docked in his jurisdiction, he inquired into who they were and where they had come from.

Indeed, they were sailors from Greece, a nation that dominated the Aegean Sea. This was why the Egyptians called Greeks "the people of the sea." Not only were they foreigners, but the ship also belonged to a Trojan royal who had been traveling with his Greek wife.

Fascinated by his discovery, Thonis headed to the temple of Hershef, where the sailors had sought sanctuary and desired to convert to the service of Hershef, thereby gaining their freedom from servitude to the Trojan prince. Their decision seemed odd to Thonis, who thought that they would want to return home above anything else.

Suspicion soon replaced curiosity, and Thonis pried deeper into the matter. The sailors confessed that they were afraid of punishment from their own gods and wanted protection from the consequences of boarding a ship with a cursed man.

The mystery gradually unraveled, and Thonis learned that the Trojan prince had stolen the wife of one of the kings in Greece—a most ignoble deed punishable by the wrath of the gods. The prince had been welcomed into the palace of the Greek king as a diplomatic guest, and yet, he repaid with evil, carting away his host's wife.

Appalled by the actions of the Greek prince, Thonis seized the ship and journeyed to the pharaoh's palace to seek the king's wisdom. Before his departure, Thonis had the Greek princess separated from the Trojan prince and escorted to the temple of Hathor, the goddess of the sky, for her safety.

Pharaoh Seti II granted Thonis an audience and promptly ordered that the Trojan prince be escorted to his presence with his converted men.

Two Lies and a Truth

The Trojan prince was a handsome man who spoke and acted like royalty. He introduced himself as Prince Paris, son of King Priam of Troy. He also revealed the Greek princess's identity as Helen, the daughter of Zeus and his new wife. According to Prince Paris, he had traveled to Sparta for the hand of Helen, which he had won fair and square, and was on his way back to Troy when the storm rerouted his ship.

The converted sailors in the hall murmured among one another, attracting the pharaoh's attention. Seti II gave them room to speak their truth on the matter, reminding them of their freedom granted by the god Hershef to speak freely.

The sailors were, however, hesitant. The prince of Troy was in the hall with them, and regardless of their new status as freemen, they did not want to go against his word.

Pharaoh Seti II took notice of their tension and promised them his protection if they spoke their truth. With this, the sailors spoke up, appraising the princess's ravishing beauty.

As it happened, the prince of Troy had indeed been a guest of Sparta, but he had not come to Sparta for Helen. In fact, the prince was not among the bachelors who had asked King Tyndareus for her hand in marriage. Also, the king had given Helen's hand to Prince Menelaus of Mycenae, not the Trojan Prince Paris, and her wedding to Menelaus had happened many years earlier. The sailor testified that the Trojan prince arrived at the gates of Sparta as an ambassador on a diplomatic mission.

The Trojan prince reportedly stayed in Sparta for the next few days. Menelaus was eventually forced to leave the city for a while on some state affairs. When he was gone, Paris carried off Helen by force, together with much treasure, and sailed away, only to be caught in a storm sent by the angry gods. His boat was swept by a violent tempest to the shores of Egypt.

Prince Paris blatantly denied having forced Helen to leave her husband and home, but the sailors insisted that they spoke the truth. There was no reason for a royal to tell lies, but the sailors sounded equally convincing.

The pharaoh, however, noted variations in the Trojan prince's story. First, he had claimed to have won Helen's hand, but after the sailors' testimony, he claimed that she had escaped with him of her own accord from a loveless marriage to King Menelaus.

Which was it?

From the Horse's Mouth

Caught in his own web of inconsistencies, the prince could no longer speak. As it stood, only one person could tell the truth: the Greek princess, Helen herself. She was safely sheltered in the temple of Hathor.

Pharaoh Seti II offered Prince Paris accommodations in the royal guest house and put his vizier, Paraemheb, in charge of the Trojan prince's welfare. Meanwhile, he would visit the Greek princess lodged in the temple and find out the truth.

With his chief priest and a trusted scribe, the king of Egypt graced the temple of Hathor with his presence and saw Helen for the first time. She was the most beautiful woman in the world. He could easily see how she was the daughter of Zeus.

Helen of Troy by Evelyn De Morgan.
https://commons.wikimedia.org/wiki/File:Helen_of_Troy.jpg

During their private conversation, Princess Helen told her story. Contrary to the Trojan prince's account, she had been happily married to Menelaus, Prince of Mycenae in Greece. She even had two children, Hermione and Nicostraus. Prince Paris had indeed forced her to come away with him after seducing her by taking the form of her husband, Menelaus.

Helen's story confirmed the sailors' version, and the Greek princess begged the pharaoh to save her from her captor, as she felt no affection for him. He was the one obsessed with her and had kidnapped her from her home.

Menelaus had been the suitor chosen by Helen's father, King Tyndareus. The prince of Troy was not even among the men who had sought the Greek princess's hand in marriage; he also did not win her hand fair and square as he had said.

It saddened the pharaoh to hear of Helen's ordeal, and he promised to send the Trojan prince away so that he would not trouble her any longer. It had been the will of the gods to intercept Helen's kidnapper and send the ship to the shores of Egypt. Urgently, the pharaoh sent word to Prince Paris and urged him to sail away from Egypt at the break of dawn. Paris's words had been proven to be lies, but because he was royalty, the pharaoh offered Prince Paris a chance to leave willingly.

The Trojan prince was unhappy to learn of the pharaoh's resolution. He swore that he would come back for Helen since she was his rightful wife. Meanwhile, on the night before his departure, the temple of Hathor (where Helen was hosted) received a divine visitation: a messenger from the sun god Ra.

His name was Thoth.

The Revelation

Thoth appeared to Tausert, Princess of Egypt and High Priestess of the goddess Hathor who lived in the temple. Tausert was so overwhelmed by the presence of Ra's messenger that she fell to her knees. She heard him speak:

"I come hither to work the will of the most high god Amon-Re [Ra], father of us all—and by his command you, who shall one day be Queen of Egypt, must learn of all that is performed this night so that you may bear witness of it in the days to come, when that king of the Aquaiusha [Greece] who is the true husband of Helen shall come to lead her home...

But this night I, whom the Aquaiusha [Greeks] name Hermes the Thrice Great, must draw forth the Ka, the double of Helen, the ghostly likeness of her that shall deceive all eyes and seem to Paris and to all at Troy to be none other than the real woman. For the Ka of Helen and not for Helen herself shall the great war of Troy be fought and the will of the Father of Gods and Men shall be accomplished."

War was coming to Greece—one that would be told and retold throughout the ages. A historic war that would end in victory for the Greeks and a crushing defeat for the city of Troy, Prince Paris's homeland. Most significantly, the war would be fought because of Helen or rather her clone.

This secret, which was revealed to Tausert, High Priestess of Hathor, was not meant for just anyone to hear. Tausert vowed to take the secret to her grave, and Thoth got to work on designing the perfect lookalike of the Greek princess.

The Trojan prince was getting ready to set sail on the Nile when Helen's clone appeared. Unknown to him, the real Helen was still in the temple of Hathor. Prince Paris was excited to have his wife back, and he hurried on his way out of Egypt before the pharaoh changed his mind.

Days rolled into months, and true to the word of Ra's messenger, the Greeks marched to war against Troy due to the actions of Prince Paris. It was a great insult to Menelaus that his wife had been stolen by a guest, and after diplomatic attempts at resolving the conflict failed, the gates of Troy were laid siege.

Menelaus enlisted the help of his older brother, King Agamemnon of Mycenae, for his offensive against Troy. They were joined by the famous war hero Achilles, the sage Odysseus, and other great soldiers, such as Ajax and Nestor. Over one thousand warships from all over Greece sailed across the vast Aegean to contend with Troy and bring Helen back.

It was just as Thoth had told Tausert that night at the temple.

The Trojans were a formidable enemy, and their people were safe behind their high city walls. For a decade, the war would go on, seemingly with no end in sight—all for what was a mere clone of the Greek princess.

Age to Age

Back in Egypt, the people were ignorant of how Helen had come to reside in the temple of Hathor. But because of her beauty and the mystery behind her existence in Egypt, the people thought her to be a human manifestation of the goddess Hathor.

The news spread throughout Memphis and all of Egypt that Hathor had taken the form of a beautiful woman and had descended into the temple to live among the mortals. The people of Egypt flocked to see Helen, whom they referred to as Hathor.

Pharaoh Seti II, who had graciously hosted the Greek princess in his kingdom, soon passed away, and the two pharaohs who came after him reigned for short periods.

Pharaoh Setnakhe, who came third after Seti II, was the first pharaoh of the Twentieth Dynasty. Like Seti II, he was kind to the Greek princess, who had not aged a day as the years whirled by. Unfortunately, Setnakhe reigned for barely three years, after which his stalwart son, Ramesses III, was enthroned.

Ramesses III was different from the other pharaohs who had ruled since Helen's circumstantial arrival in Egypt. It had been almost twenty years, and yet her beauty was unchanging. Ramesses III took one look at Helen and wanted her for himself.

Despite Queen Tausert's pleas that he cease desiring another man's wife, Ramesses III was unmoved in his lust for her. Tausert, who had been the high priestess of Hathor since the time of Helen's arrival, feared that the pharaoh's desire was a recipe for disaster.

Tausert prayed earnestly to Hathor for a solution, and one day, the answer to her prayers docked on the shores of Canopus near the temple.

The Reunion

Helen rushed out of her residence when she heard the news.

She prayed to Hathor that it be true; she had waited for so long. A man stood at the temple entrance, wearing a tired yet happy smile: Menelaus.

There was no containing the Greek princess's joy at being reunited with her husband. Menelaus took her in his arms, entranced and full of stories to tell his wife.

After all those years of war against Troy, the Greeks realized that there was no destroying the Trojans from the outside. Their best soldiers, even the mighty Achilles, had died in the war, and the Greeks were distraught. So, they devised a clever plot to get into the city walls of Troy.

At the behest of Odysseus, one of the wisest men on Menelaus's side, they built a large wooden horse, set it on the shores of Troy, and vanished without a trace. The Trojans came out of their fortress and wondered what the horse was about. The Greeks had left a message for them, stating that they had surrendered and returned to their homeland since the city of Troy was so impenetrable. They had tired of war. The gigantic wooden horse was their symbol of surrender.

The Trojans were initially suspicious, but with no Greek soldier or ship in sight for miles, their doubts faded away. They rolled the large wooden horse into the city, and King Priam of Troy threw an elaborate party to celebrate their victory over the Greeks.

Unknown to the Trojans, there were hundreds of Greek soldiers hiding inside the horse that they had just brought into the city. After a long night of drinking and merrymaking, the Trojans drifted off to sleep. While they snored and slumbered, the Greeks came out of their hiding and opened the city gates for the rest of their troops. Troy was mercilessly sacked, and Menelaus recovered his wife (Helen's clone).

The Trojan Horse.
Adam Jones from Kelowna, BC, Canada, CC BY-SA 2.0
https://creativecommons.org/licenses/by-sa/2.0 via Wikimedia Commons;
https://commons.wikimedia.org/wiki/File:Replica_of_Trojan_Horse_-
_Canakkale_Waterfront_-_Dardanelles_-_Turkey_(5747677790).jpg

Menelaus continued with his story, telling Helen that he had been on his way home from Troy with Helen (the clone) when an unforgiving storm wrecked his ship. The clone Helen had vanished in the process, and Menelaus had thought his wife had surely died.

He fell apart in sorrow and was on the verge of committing suicide when the gods revealed to him that the real Helen was safe in Egypt in the temple of Hathor. Prince Paris had recovered a mere clone made by the gods. The Trojan War had been fought over a fake.

Menelaus expressed his bedazzlement at Egyptian magic, and he thanked High Priestess Tausert for keeping his wife safe. He also learned of Pharaoh Ramesses III's rather disturbing plans to marry Helen. The pharaoh had asked her hand in marriage and was on his way for her answer. He had threatened to take her by force if she dared refuse him. So, Helen's husband had returned in the nick of time.

Queen Tausert was not only the priestess of Hathor, but she was also Ramesses's mother. Yet, she promised to help Menelaus and his wife escape safely from Egypt. Running away would raise the ruler's ire, so Tausert came up with a better plan.

The Escape Route

It was a fine evening in Egypt. The pharaoh was in high spirits, anticipating a positive response from the beautiful woman who lived in Hathor's temple. His arrival at the temple was grand and elaborate, but the welcome was short of befitting.

Instead of an excited bride-to-be, Ramesses found Helen dressed in mourning clothes and an unkempt, weary-looking traveler saying words of comfort to her. The king's mother, Tausert, was also there, and the mood in the room was sorrowful.

The king of Egypt demanded to be informed of the situation, and Tausert did the talking. The man comforting Helen was a sailor from Menelaus's boat, which had been destroyed at sea during a turbulent storm. Ramesses questioned the sailor, who, unknown to him, was Menelaus. When the sailor confirmed that he had seen Menelaus's corpse at sea with his own eyes, the pharaoh did not hide his delight. Now, there was no reason for Helen to decline to marry him.

Right there and then, Ramesses asked Helen to marry him. She agreed, but she gave a small condition: the pharaoh would allow her some time to mourn her late husband in accordance with Greek customs. She requested a ship, one well provisioned with the food and wine needed for a good funeral feast. Helen also requested to have all the treasures the Trojan prince had stolen, as well as a bull to sacrifice to the spirit of her husband.

In addition, she requested the pharaoh's permission to take the sailors who had revealed the truth to him. She would need them to perform the funerary rites and sacrifices for her late husband.

She told the pharaoh, "I must accompany them to speak the words and pour the last offering to my husband's spirit—and all this must be done on the sea in which his body lies, for then only can his spirit find rest in the realm of Hades—and only then can I be your bride."

Ramesses saw no reason to refuse, but this was only because he did not realize he was being tricked. With the pharaoh's consent, Helen and Menelaus sailed away from Egypt, never again to return. The couple had traveled far beyond reach before Ramesses learned the truth. In a fit of rage, he sought to kill his mother, Tausert, for masterminding the Greek princess's escape.

That night, Thoth appeared to Pharaoh Ramesses and told him that Tausert had acted in accordance with the will of the gods. The king could do his mother no harm then or after.

Some refer to the myth of the Greek princess as the Egyptian version of the Trojan War. The more commonly known Greek version differs quite a bit. The Egyptian myth is a tale of the predestined journey of a divine mortal and how Egypt was a refuge for her while one of history's most epic wars raged across the Aegean.

Chapter 9 – The Treasure Thief

This story begins after the Greek Princess Helen evaded an unwanted marriage to Pharaoh Ramesses III and fled with her husband, Menelaus.

After being cautioned by the gods to bring no harm to his mother, Tausert, the king of Egypt refocused on the politics and economy of his kingdom. In the years that followed, Egypt prospered considerably under Ramesses III. Not only had he conquered the invaders from Libya, Palestine, and other nations along the Mediterranean Sea in his early regnal years, the king of Egypt had established a trade network with neighboring countries to foster harmonious relations.

This helped replenish the coffers in Egypt, which had previously been depleted during the constant wars against foreign aggression. Pharaoh Ramesses not only sought the prosperity of Egypt, but he also desired tremendous wealth of his own. To this end, he began to collect his riches in weights of gold, silver, and gems.

Treasure Bank

One day, the king awoke with a brilliant idea to preserve his fortune. He immediately summoned his finest builder, a man named Horemheb, to share his thoughts. The king envisioned a secret stash for all his wealth, which he fortified against thieves and burglars. Horemheb was delighted to learn of the king's plan and offered himself to receive the king's instructions.

Pharaoh Ramesses ordered his builder to construct a fortress of stone with thick, impenetrable walls and a roof as high as the pyramids. This would be the king's treasure cave, and it would be guarded heavily by soldiers. By then, the king had other construction projects going on, including his magnificent temple in the hills of Thebes, along the western bank of the Nile River.

Horemheb took the king's command and enacted it. He hired the best stoneworkers in all of Egypt, and they mined the best stones from the quarries of Swenett (later called Syene). With these stones, the king's treasure bank was erected, and as Horemheb had promised, it was nothing like any such edifice before it. Its doors were constructed from the finest quality stone, and the inner chamber doors were made of bronze and iron.

Pleased with Horemheb's fine work, Pharaoh Ramesses rewarded him and had all his treasures moved to their new home. The doors to the treasure chamber were sealed shut by the king himself, and he returned to the palace, assured of the safety of his wealth.

What the king didn't know was that his treasures were far from safe.

<u>Mission Impossible</u>

It was night, and all through the land, there was peace and quiet. All of Egypt was asleep, except the men stationed to guard the pharaoh's treasure—and two other men.

They were on a secret, dangerous mission, one that would lead to their deaths if they were discovered. They had slipped past the king's guards and let themselves in through a secret entrance. Now, they were filling their sacks with their share of the loot.

The two men operated in silence and took only a little of the abundance in the room, just as they had the last time and the time before that—and all the many times before that. The king's treasure was visibly reduced, but the thieves would not stop until they had carted away enough or maybe even all of it.

Morning came, and they vanished without a trace, save for the king's missing treasures. Pharaoh Ramesses stormed to his treasure bank and discovered that he had once again been robbed. He was furious. He had lost count of how many times these thieves had made away with his precious fortune.

The only man who knew the intricacies of his treasure bank was the one who had built it: Horemheb. But Horemheb was long dead after completing the construction. He had passed away after a terrible sickness afflicted him.

Who were these thieves, and how had they gotten in so many times without breaking the seal or getting caught by the king's guards?

The pharaoh had had enough of these mysterious delinquents. He needed a plan to catch them in the act and punish them severely. For days, he pondered on a solution, and then it occurred to him: traps.

The robbers were sneaky, like rats, and what better way to catch rats than with strategically positioned traps?

*

It was another perfect night to steal from the king's fortune.

The two sons of Horemheb crept their way into the king's treasure bank and took the secret pathway that their father, Horemheb, had revealed to them on his deathbed shortly before he died. Unknown to the king, the man he had trusted to build his treasure fortress had installed a tiny pathway through the walls to access his fortune. Before his death, Horemheb had summoned his two sons and handed them the mandate of plundering the king's fortune.

It was another night to embark on this deadly mission. There was no getting enough of the king's treasure, and so they had come to steal some more. Unknown to Horemheb's sons, the king had anticipated their move and set a deadly trap inside the treasure chamber near the chests of gold and silver.

The brothers snuck in, wading through the darkness to get to their prize. But one of the brothers fell into the king's trap. He struggled to free himself, but it was of no use. He was going to bleed out. His identity would be revealed. Or worse, he would be captured half-dead and cruelly tortured into naming his accomplice.

To protect himself, his brother, and his family, the trapped brother pleaded for his brother to kill him and cut off his head. That way, he would die painlessly, and with his head gone, no one would recognize his corpse.

The brother blatantly refused. There had to be some other way. He dropped to his knees and attempted to free his entrapped brother several times and in several different ways, but his efforts were futile. The entrapped brother fervently repeated his request and added that they were running out of time. If they were both caught, they would both have to pay with their lives in the most humiliating way.

Hesitantly, the other brother granted the entrapped brother his wish of an honor killing and decapitated him. Afterward, he slipped out of the king's treasure chamber and took his brother's severed head and clothes with him to bury.

The Ultimate Outwitter

Pharaoh Ramesses III was stirred when he heard of the headless unclad corpse caught in his trap. His guards denied being responsible for his death, and whoever did it had expertly left no traces. The seals on the doors remained unbroken, and there were no other signs of a breach.

The king of Egypt took this as a personal challenge, and he garnered his every resolve to outwit the cunning thief. Ramesses could recognize an honor killing when he saw one, and the only way to root out any accomplices was by using the headless corpse.

When morning came, the people murmured among themselves. Those who walked past the palace gates that morning reported a most sordid sight. A naked, headless corpse dangled on a rope in front of the palace. It didn't sound like the body would come down anytime soon, as it was done on the king's orders.

The second brother heard the rumors and had to find out if they were true. They were. His brother's corpse was hung in front of the palace as part of the king's plan to catch him. The king had also stationed his soldiers to observe the reactions of all who saw the corpse. It was highly likely that a family member would come around, see his kinsman hanging, and be unable to contain their sorrow. If such a person turned up at the palace gates to grieve or claim the body, the king had ordered his soldiers to arrest him immediately.

However, the second brother saw through the king's plan, and he decided that he would not fall for it. However, matters quickly became complicated when his mother heard of the gruesome display of her son's corpse. She was maddened with grief and shouted at her other son, ordering him to bring home his brother's corpse. Otherwise, he would never enter the Duat.

The second brother had not anticipated that his mother would cause such a ruckus, and he attempted to comfort her. He assured her that he had properly buried his brother's head with their deceased father and that it was enough for the dead brother to enter the gates of the Duat. But his mother remained thoroughly unconvinced. She cried out louder and threatened to expose his secret to the pharaoh. She was ready to accept whatever consequences came with it, even if it meant the death of her son.

The other brother could perceive that his mother was set in her demands, and he promised to bring home his brother's corpse. He thought up another brilliant scheme.

*

The pharaoh had never been so furious.

How could his own men be so reckless and incompetent as to get drunk while on duty? The men sobered up and explained in detail what had transpired the evening before. An elderly merchant had passed by the palace with two donkeys loaded with wineskins. His donkeys had collided, and their harnesses tore two wineskins open. The wine in the skins leaked out, and the merchant was so upset that he cried out loudly, attracting the soldiers' attention.

Rather than let the wine go to waste, the soldiers helped themselves to the full batches of wine that leaked from the wineskins. The merchant sat with them and shared another wineskin, and they guzzled it greedily. Eventually, they became drunk and drifted off into a deep sleep.

By morning, the merchant had disappeared, and so had the corpse the guards had been assigned to watch over. The merchant had been the second brother, and his plan had worked better than he could have imagined.

Hearing the details made the pharaoh even angrier. He condemned the erring soldiers to a severe flogging and had them dragged out of his sight. Ramesses clenched his fists on his throne, enraged by the audacity of this common thief. He became even more determined to catch this lawbreaker.

It was time to roll out another plan.

*

Another dawn broke in the land of Egypt, and there was fresh news being whispered in the streets. There was an important visitor in the land, and she was the most beautiful woman to arrive on the shores of Egypt after Helen. This woman was an eligible bachelorette, and her hand in marriage would go to any man who told her the best secret.

The men of Egypt trooped to the camp where the beauty was lodged and took turns to win her hand in marriage. The living brother was one of them, and when it was his turn, he saw that she was very beautiful indeed. Even though it was dark, her radiance could not be denied. She offered him a seat and proceeded to ask him about the secret she wanted him to tell. "Tell me the wickedest and cleverest things you have ever done."

If the lady was fascinated by his answer, she would consent to marry him. For the second brother, the answer to this was obvious, so he told it to her. He had beheaded his own brother, who had been caught in the king's trap while they were stealing the king's treasure.

The woman suddenly screamed aloud, alerting her guards that she had caught the treasure thief. She grabbed the second brother's hand and held on to it until the king's guards arrived. But when they turned on the lights, he had vanished. What the woman was holding on to was the severed hand of his dead brother.

Horrified, she screamed and let go of the hand. As it turned out, she was no stranger in the land of Egypt. She was the king's daughter, the princess of Egypt, and like her father, she had been tricked by a man who knew all about their plan.

She returned to the palace and told her father what had happened. This time, the king had a different reaction. He had obsessed so long and hard over catching the treasure thief that he had missed the bigger picture.

The thief was a man of rare genius, and his foresight was second to none. It would be a colossal waste of his talents to punish him. Pharaoh Ramesses issued a decree that announced a pardon for the treasure thief's crimes and a promise of rich rewards if he would join the king's service as a retainer.

In a most unlikely end, the second brother finally revealed himself to the king, and he was given a title in the king's court. He also married the princess of Egypt and never again had to sneak into the king's treasure house.

Chapter 10 – The Tale of Hatshepsut

"A people of ignoble origin from the East, whose country was unforeseen, had the audacity to invade the country, which they had mastered by main force without difficulty or even battle. Having overpowered the chiefs, they then savagely burnt the cities, razed the temples of the gods to the grounds, and treated the whole native population with the utmost cruelty, massacring some, and carrying off the wives and children of others into slavery."

This is the widely debated account of an Egyptian historian named Manetho. In that passage, he describes the Hyksos invasion of Egypt in the 1600s BCE. While modern historians argue that these foreigners took over parts of Egypt as peacefully as possible, lore remains loyal to Manetho's account.

Egypt was reportedly plundered by these Semitic foreigners, and trade routes were disrupted, leaving the succeeding pharaohs struggling to regain Egypt's power. This story is about an unusual pharaoh whose reign is celebrated in history as one of restoration and development.

This pharaoh ascended to the throne of Egypt amid unfavorable odds and left an indelible mark on Egyptian history. This pharaoh was a woman, and her name was Hatshepsut.

The Royally Divine

Set in the Eighteenth Dynasty of Egypt, the story of Hatshepsut mythically begins with the sun god Ra's decision to enthrone a great woman as the pharaoh of Egypt and give her the whole world. The sun god's grand plan would be brought to fruition through the body of a beautiful woman named Ahmose, wife of Pharaoh Thutmose and the queen of Egypt.

The sun god commissioned Thoth to arrange the conception of a baby girl that would grow up to become the pharaoh of Egypt. Thoth obliged and descended to Earth during the night. He headed into the palace. His divine task could not be discovered, so he spelled every mortal in the palace to sleep deeply and possessed the body of Pharaoh Thutmose.

The possessed pharaoh trudged to his queen's bedchamber and found her sound asleep on her lion-shaped couch. The king moved to her and held her up, breathing the divine breath of Ra into her nostrils. He also blessed her and declared that the child that would be born would rule the two lands of Egypt.

Queen Ahmose thought it was all a dream, but she soon gave birth to a beautiful baby girl. She was named Hatshepsut, and the king's household celebrated her arrival in grand style. That night, another divine visitation was paid to the palace. This time, the sun god Ra himself came down, accompanied by the goddess Hathor and her seven daughters (known as the Seven Hathors). The sun god took the baby princess and gave her the kiss of power and his blessing to rule Egypt.

The Takeover

Hatshepsut had the typical upbringing of an Egyptian princess. She was taught to prioritize her familial and sacred duties above all else. She would likely become the wife of a pharaoh and nothing more.

It was unheard of for a woman to become the pharaoh of Egypt. The throne had always been occupied by men, save for Sobekneferu, who had reigned for barely four years with little known achievements.

When Pharaoh Thutmose passed away around 1493 BCE, his son, Thutmose II, became the king of Egypt. Hatshepsut was married off to her brother, Thutmose II, at the age of twelve and became the queen of Egypt. This was a common practice in ancient Egypt, and the new king and queen would reign for the next few years.

Hatshepsut bore a daughter for the King, Princess Neferure, but it seemed she was unable to have any sons. Having an heir was important to the continuation of the dynasty, and no chances could be taken. Eventually, a woman from the pharaoh's harem, who went by the name Iset, gave birth to an heir for the king.

The prince was named Thutmose III, and Queen Hatshepsut adopted him as her stepson. Thutmose III was almost three years old when his father, the king, suddenly died, leaving him next in line for the throne.

Evidently, the prince was too young to be entrusted with affairs of governance and needed a guardian, also known as a regent. Queen Hatshepsut stepped forward and became Thutmose III's regent around 1479 BCE.

In time, Hatshepsut understood what her divine mandate was. She was to be more than this. Beyond the spiritual, she was an ambitious woman who knew all about the state of Egypt and the struggle to recover from the Hyksos invasion that had happened long before she was born. One day, Hatshepsut learned of a plot by the other royal families to usurp the throne from her stepson. This would bring the reign of the Eighteenth Dynasty to an abrupt end.

Hatshepsut would not allow the throne of Egypt to be snatched from her family line, so in the fifth to seventh regnal year of the young Thutmose III, Hatshepsut assumed the throne of Egypt as pharaoh.

The people of Egypt woke up to the most unprecedented news. They had a new king; it was a woman. Aware of her uncanny rise to the throne of Egypt, Pharaoh Hatshepsut proceeded to legitimize her reign by declaring herself the intended heir of her father, the deceased Pharaoh Thutmose I. She handpicked trusted retainers to fill the important positions of government, notably Senenmut, an architect and Pharaoh Hatshepsut's rumored lover.

Next, Pharaoh Hatshepsut tried to convince the people that she was ordained by the gods as the one to unite the two lands of Egypt and restore the country to its former glory. As proof of this, she adopted the name Maatkare, which means "Truth is the soul of the sun god." She also underwent purification rites and observances during her coronation and wore crowns that represented Upper and Lower Egypt.

Before succeeding to the throne, Hatshepsut had only been known as a princess and then queen of Egypt. Her new elevated status required her to carve a new image in the eyes of her people. So, Hatshepsut took things a step further by ordering to be dressed and addressed as a man in person and in pictorial depictions. She took to wearing the male kingly regalia and being portrayed as having a fake beard and a muscular build. She was referenced with respect as "His Majesty."

The Sphinx of Hatshepsut showing her fake beard.

Hatshepsut: The Builder and Trader

Hatshepsut knew that changing her wardrobe was not all there was to be a great pharaoh. One day, she summoned Minister Senenmut and tasked him with overseeing her greatest building projects. Conversely, she embarked on the historic expedition to Punt to revive trade in Egypt.

Many pharaohs before Hatshepsut had shown little commitment to construction projects outside of tombs or pyramids. After the Hyksos had "savagely" invaded Egypt, many temples and monuments were destroyed, leaving the cultural heritage of the land in shambles.

The buildings that Pharaoh Hatshepsut had in mind were no basic relics. She envisioned grand and magnificent structures that would outlive her and become a legacy for many generations. After she consulted with Senenmut, it was agreed that Ineni, an aristocratic architect who had served the past two pharaohs, would be best for the job.

Construction began in multiple locations throughout Upper and Lower Egypt. The Temple of Karnak, which had multiple shrines dedicated to the worship of the Egyptian goddess of the earth, Mut (the Precinct of Mut), was renovated. The Precinct of Mut had fallen to the Hyksos in the Eleventh Dynasty, and its prominence had dwindled over time. With the reconstruction sponsored by Pharaoh Hatshepsut, the Precinct of Mut regained prestige.

Also, in Karnak, Hatshepsut built the Chapelle Rouge, also known as the Red Chapel. This shrine was built in honor of Ra, and it housed the sacred golden barque believed to transport the sun god on his journeys. On festival days, the statue of Ra would be mounted on the barque and carried out of the Karnak shrine by a procession of priests through the streets of Thebes. He would be returned after the festivities. The interior of the shrine was decorated with reliefs and epigraphs of the prosperous reign of the pharaoh.

The Temple of Pakhet, which honored the goddesses Baset and Sekhmet, was also constructed by Pharaoh Hatshepsut as a gesture to revive Egyptian culture. This temple was commissioned in Beni Hasan and came to be renamed the Cave of Artemis by the Greeks (this was because Artemis was the Greek equivalent of Baset and Sekhmet).

Hatshepsut was also famous for her obelisks. At her behest, High Steward Amenhotep saw to the erection of twin obelisks at the entrance of the Temple of Karnak. At the time, they were the tallest in the world. The pharaoh would have two more obelisks built to mark the celebration of her sixteenth regnal year and a third to replace one of her obelisks in Aswan that had crumbled after its initial construction.

One of Pharaoh Hatshepsut's obelisks at Karnak.
PirouzZ, CC BY-SA 4.0 https://creativecommons.org/licenses/by-sa/4.0 via Wikimedia Commons:
https://commons.wikimedia.org/wiki/File:Obelisk_of_Hatshepsut_at_Karnak.jpg

Also significant was the construction of Pharaoh Hatshepsut's grand royal tomb along the west bank of the Nile near Luxor. This site was called Deir el-Bahri, and it would become the entry point to the famous Valley of the Kings. Hatshepsut's royal tomb was also a temple, a complex titled the "Holy of Holies" or Djeser-Djeseru. It was a majestic structure that stood out from the rest because of its lovely gardens and layered terraces, ornamented with statues of Osiris and Hatshepsut, as well as an avenue of sphinxes out front. Mortuary temples in ancient Egypt were designed to honor the sun god and for the posthumous worship of the pharaoh who built them.

Not only was Pharaoh Hatshepsut a master builder, but her reign is also credited with the largest ancient Egyptian trade expedition in history. Following the aggressive occupation of the Hyksos, Egypt had lost plenty of temples and statues. The country's coffers were adversely affected, and the pharaoh sought to replenish Egypt's wealth.

In the ninth year of her reign, five ships departed Egypt in the name of Pharaoh Hatshepsut. Their destination was an African land across the Red Sea called Punt. Prior to the invasion of the Hyksos, the land of Punt had a long history of trade with Egypt, dating back as far as the Fifth Dynasty. One day, the pharaoh heard of Punt and all its riches. It was such a "beautiful land" that the people called it the Land of the Gods.

Pharaoh Hatshepsut charged a Nubian chancellor named Nehsi to lead her ships on a trading mission to Punt. The pharaoh's delegation was well received by the royals of Punt, and their mission was successful. They returned to Egypt with items of ebony, savory resin, ivory, frankincense, gold, and myrrh. Live myrrh trees were harvested from Punt and brought back to Egypt to be planted in the pharaoh's mortuary temple. The pharaoh herself discovered burned frankincense was a useful ingredient in the production of kohl or eye makeup.

While peaceful trade was the theme of Pharaoh Hatshepsut's foreign policy, there are indications that she led strictly military campaigns to Byblos, Canaan, Nubia, and the Sinai Peninsula.

Despite the efforts of erasing her legacy embarked upon by Hatshepsut's successor, Thutmose III, the tale of Pharaoh Hatshepsut and her greatness has survived for generations. She was ordained by divinity, and her tenure restored the wealth and eminence of Egypt.

Chapter 11 – The Doomed Prince

This story begins with the agony of a king without an heir.

He was the king of all Egypt, worshiped as the son of Ra and the father of his people. Yet, he had no son to continue his royal line. Every night, the king would pray earnestly to the gods to make his wife fertile and bear him a son. He also gave many offerings to appease the gods of fertility. One day, he received a promise that his wife would bear a son. And so, she did.

The king called a grand celebration in honor of the gods for answering his prayers. As was the norm, the royal family consulted with the Seven Hathors, deities revered as knowing mortals' fates. They needed to hear what the prince's fate would be.

Unfortunately, the Seven Hathors foretold that a horrible untimely death would befall the prince. He would be killed by a crocodile, dog, or snake.

When the king heard this, he was sorely afraid. He mourned the fate of his son along with his queen. He was as good as heirless, and there was almost no changing their fate. However, the king of Egypt was willing to take his chances.

He immediately ordered for a fortress to be built in the mountains for the prince to live in. It was made from the finest materials in the land and furnished to royal taste. Everything the young prince needed to live in comfort and luxury was provided in the fortress, and the prince was moved there to live out his childhood.

The years passed, and as the prince grew, his curiosity about the world beyond the walls around him grew. He would look from the top of the roof at the horizon, unable to tell what the world felt like. One day, he saw a strange creature wandering outside the walls. He had never seen it before, but it was nothing like a man or a woman.

The young prince asked one of his servants what it was, and he learned that it was a dog. The prince was fascinated by it, and he petitioned his father to let him possess one. The king refused, remembering the prophecy of the Seven Hathors, but the prince was unrelenting until his desire was fulfilled.

That was not the end of it. The prince demanded to know the reason behind his imprisonment and why he could not live with his family.

The king and queen realized that the time had come to tell the prince his destiny. The prince received the knowledge of his fate with bravery. He asked that he be allowed to explore the world for the rest of his days on Earth. The king and queen were reluctant to send off their only son into a world of uncertainty and danger, but once again, they granted him his wish.

So, the prince and his dog set off on an adventure far beyond the shores of Egypt. The prince had no destination in mind, but he went toward the east, led by his own whims. He came to Nahairana, a small town bustling with activity. It seemed to be a festival, as there were many eager young men in the streets. The prince asked one of them what the occasion was. He was told it was a contest. The men of the land were competing to win the hand of the beautiful princess.

The princess lived in a tower that was over one hundred feet high and had seventy windows. Whoever could climb to the highest room in the tower and reach the princess would be the winner of the contest and be allowed to marry her.

Many a brave young man attempted to reach the princess's elevated chamber, but none prevailed. Day after day, the prince of Egypt watched the other young men try, but the task was daunting and seemingly insurmountable.

One bright day, the prince decided to try his luck. Like the princess of Nahairana, he had also lived out his childhood in seclusion. As a result of this, he had picked up considerable climbing skills.

The prince of Egypt succeeded in his quest, but the king would not give his daughter's hand away to a fugitive from Egypt. He remained opposed to the marriage until the princess vowed to take her life if the king would not change his mind. The princess had fallen in love with the prince at first sight, and eventually, her father gave her his blessing. He also gifted servants, land, cattle, property, and precious jewels to the prince. With his new wife, the prince soon longed to return home to Egypt.

Before that, the prince opened up to his wife about the prophecy of the Seven Hathors. He was doomed to be killed by a crocodile, dog, or snake. The princess worried for the safety of her husband and suggested that his pet dog be killed. The prince declined, as the dog had been his companion since he was a boy and had not harmed him even once.

Together, the prince and his wife began their journey back to Egypt. On their way, they came to a large lake, which bordered a quaint town. This lake teemed with crocodiles, and the prince's life was in danger. With the help of a giant who resided in the town near the lake, the prince's life was saved.

The prince and his wife settled in a new home, and he was almost attacked by a snake several times. His wife and servants thwarted every attempt on the prince's life. The prince offered endless prayers and sacrifices to the gods to change his and his wife's fate, as she would be destined to live without her beloved.

One evening, the prince went out hunting with his dog. The dog caught a whiff of game in the forest and chased after it. The prince followed, ready to make his kill until his dog plunged into a nearby river. The prince halted, horrified at what was about to happen. A large crocodile emerged from the river and said, "Behold, I am thy doom, following after thee."

And here, the story ends abruptly. The ancient document where this myth is written was so badly damaged that the end of this story remains unknown.

Did the prince die as he was fated to, or did he escape the grim prophecy of the Seven Hathors?

Chapter 12 – The Two Brothers

Bata ran as fast as his legs could carry him.

As he tumbled down the narrow dusty pathway, he could hear Anpu chasing after him with a spear in hand. Only Ra himself could save Bata from being killed for a crime he did not commit.

How did it all begin?

This is the story of "The Two Brothers" from classic Egyptian mythology. It begins with the peaceful coexistence of two brothers; the older was named Anpu, and the younger was named Bata.

Anpu and Bata were born to the same parents, and as the eldest, Anpu owned a house, cattle, and land. He also had a wife, and Bata lived with them. Bata was an excellent farmer. He cultivated the land and planted and harvested crops on his brother's land. He was also the one who fed and worked the cattle. Bata had a supernatural ability to speak to animals.

Every morning, he woke up first to work the field with the oxen, feed the cattle, and bring milk and cheese home for Anpu and his wife. Anpu's farm was in the best hands in Egypt, as Bata was a man who knew of the seasons.

One day in the Season of Emergence, Bata requested Anpu to join in plowing the land. Anpu agreed, and when the next dawn broke, the two brothers went to the farm. They built ridges and planted many seeds. When they ran out of seeds, Anpu sent Bata home to fetch some more, and Bata headed urgently back.

At home, he met Anpu's wife, who was grooming her hair. Bata asked her to get him the seeds, but she declined.

"Go yourself and open the storeroom," she said. "Take whatsoever you desire. If I were to rise for you, my hair would become unruly once more."

Bata obliged and went into the storeroom. On his way out, something unexpected happened. Anpu's wife seduced him and expressed her desire to have sexual relations with him. Bata was repulsed by her advances. He said, "I regard you as a mother, and my brother is like a father to me. You have spoken evil words, and I desire not to hear them again, nor will I repeat to any man what you have spoken."

With this, Bata hurried back to the farm and worked there with Anpu until the evening. Anpu returned home to a surprising twist of events. His wife was in bad shape. She looked beaten and battered by a brute. She lay on the floor in pain, unable to light the lamp or give her husband water to wash his hands with as ancient Egyptian custom required.

Anpu held her in his arms and asked what had happened to her. Anpu's wife spoke that it was Bata who had attacked her when he came home to fetch more seeds. She accused him of threatening to kill her if she told Anpu about any of it.

His wife's words made Anpu violently angry. Armed with a sword and spear, Anpu charged to Bata's quarters to kill him. Meanwhile, Bata was in the barn with the oxen when one of them told him that his brother was on his way to kill him.

Bata peeped through the barn door, and indeed, Anpu was armed and on his way. Bata fled the farm with Anpu hot on his trail.

While running for his life, Bata said a loud prayer to Ra, asking for help and vindication.

The god heard Bata's prayer and caused a river to break out from the dry land, separating the two brothers. The river teemed with crocodiles, and Anpu could not get to Bata. From across the river, Bata declared his innocence to Anpu and told his side of the story: the truth. To further prove his innocence, Bata cut a part of himself (his penis, according to some versions of this story) and threw it into the river, where a fish ate it.

As Bata bled, Anpu was convinced, and he was full of regret. He tried to reach his brother, but he could not cross the river. Bata announced that he was headed for the Valley of Cedars, where he would cut out his heart and hang it on a cedar tree. If the tree was ever cut down, he would die. Bata charged Anpu with a seven-year quest to find his heart and put it inside a vessel of water so that he could come back to life.

Afterward, he bade Anpu farewell and went on his way. Full of regret and anguish, Anpu returned home and killed his wife.

Bata's Woman

Bata found a home in the Valley of Cedars, where he encountered the Ennead of Heliopolis. Ra took pity on Bata for his plight and instructed the god Khnum to create a wife for the man so he would not be lonely anymore.

Bata's new wife was divinely beautiful, and there was no other woman like her in all of Egypt. The Seven Hathors appeared on the scene and looked at her. As the knowers of fate, they foretold that Bata's wife would live a short life. They foretold of her death, just as they had in the myth of the doomed prince.

Sorely afraid of losing his wife, Bata resolved to protect his wife with his last breath. She would not step outside the house or go near the sea or into the forest. This remained the norm for many months until one day, the king of Egypt heard of her and sought her hand in marriage.

He sent countless messengers to deliver his intention to Bata's wife until she agreed to meet him. The king fell in love with Bata's wife and married her, despite knowing that she belonged to another man. When Bata's wife revealed her husband's secret about his heart hanging on a cedar tree, the king sent his soldiers to cut the tree down. Bata died.

A Reunion of Brothers

Anpu got the sign to start his quest and rescue his brother. He darted off to the Valley of Cedars and found Bata in his house, lifeless. Anpu set out to find his brother's heart or some other way to bring him back to life. After four years, he found a seed that had Bata's soul inside it.

He took the seed and dropped it into a jar of water, and Bata came back. He was alive. Anpu restored Bata's soul by having him drink the water with the seed inside it. Bata was revived, and the two brothers joyfully embraced.

Bata transformed into a bull, and Anpu rode it to the palace. The king was so delighted at the creature's display of magical powers that he made it a sacred bull in the temple and rewarded Anpu in gold and silver for it. As a bull, Bata revealed himself to his wife, and she was terrified yet unremorseful for revealing his secret to the king.

Instead, the queen petitioned the king to slaughter the sacred bull and permit her to eat its liver. Bound by an oath to grant whatever she desired, the king reluctantly agreed. The sacred bull—Bata—was sacrificed.

While it was being killed, two drops of the sacred bull's blood fell to the ground, and two magnificent Persea trees sprouted from them. The king's attendants marveled at this mystery and told the king of it. The king pronounced the trees to be sacred.

Again, Bata, in the form of the sacred trees, revealed himself to the queen. She went pale with fright and tricked the king once more into swearing an oath to grant her desire. Then, she asked for the sacred Persea trees to be cut down. The king was unable to refuse. He assigned the most skilled lumberjacks in Egypt to cut the tree down, and they began, with the queen watching. Unknown to her, a tiny splinter from the trees entered her mouth, and she swallowed it.

This splinter caused the queen to become pregnant, and she soon birthed a son, thinking him to be the pharaoh's son. Unknown to the king and queen, the boy was an incarnation of Bata, and he would inherit the Kingdom of Egypt after their death.

When Bata became the king of Egypt, he summoned his brother Anpu and made him next in line to the throne of Egypt. The two brothers were united once more, never to be separated again.

Chapter 13 – Isis and the Seven Scorpions

It was a chilly evening, and the murky marshes of the Nile were no place for a mother and her infant child. Her clothes were no better than rags, and memories of her imprisonment in that spinning mill plagued her mind.

This mysterious woman had an unusual company of bodyguards. They were not able-bodied men or even gods. They were gigantic venomous scorpions. There were seven of them, and they formed a protective circle around her as she made for a mansion on the horizon.

The seven scorpions were named Tefen, Masetetef, Petet, Tjetet, Matet, Mesetet, and Befen. They were assigned by Serket at the behest of the god Thoth to protect the woman and her child from harm. They soon arrived at the mansion, and when the woman knocked desperately, the doors of the mansion opened.

There stood Usert, a wealthy woman who owned and lived in the mansion.

Repulsed by her haggard appearance, Usert showed no compassion for the woman or her baby. Instead, she slammed her door in the faces of these unwanted guests and walked away without remorse.

Little did she know that it was no mere mortal at her door. It was the great and powerful goddess Isis, and her baby was Horus, son of Osiris. Our myth of Isis and the Seven Scorpions is set after the gruesome murder of Osiris and the usurpation of the Egyptian throne by the evil god Set.

Set was on a rampage to wipe out Osiris's bloodline forever, but Thoth, in his wisdom, had helped protect Isis and her son, who was destined to avenge his father. After her escape, Isis concealed her divinity by taking on the form of an ordinary woman to avoid being discovered by Set's hunting dogs.

After being disparaged by Usert, Isis headed for a village behind the mansion to seek help, but her companions, the seven scorpions, would not forgive the insult.

Isis found refuge in the humble home of a poor fisher girl who had only a straw bed and simple food to offer. It was more than enough for Isis and her baby, and they spent the night there, contented.

Meanwhile, the aggrieved companions of Isis held a meeting that night and concocted the ultimate revenge for Usert's insult. One after another, the scorpions transferred all their venom to their leader Tefen and sent him to the mansion.

While the people in the village slept, Tefen crawled in the dead of night and went into Usert's house. The scorpion found Usert's son sound asleep in his chamber and stung him hard. The next morning, Usert found her son on the verge of death. She grabbed him and rushed into the city, crying and seeking help.

Isis was tending to her baby when she heard the ruckus. She was moved with pity for the dying child, and when no one could save him from his suffering, she offered aid.

The boy was in severe pain since the poison in his body tortured him. He cried out in agony. Isis knew that it was the work of her scorpions and took the boy in her arms. She called out each scorpion by name and neutralized its poison in the boy's body with her potent spells.

The goddess then revealed herself to Usert, the one who had rejected her. She also revealed herself to the fisher girl who had shown her generosity. Usert was overcome with guilt and remorse for failing to recognize Isis and being so unwelcoming. She thanked Isis for saving her son and gave all her wealth to the poor fisher girl as a gesture of worship. The myth of Isis and the Seven Scorpions is popular in Egypt since it hinges on kindness, patience, compassion, and forgiveness.

Chapter 14 – The Prince and the Sphinx

The story of the Prince and the Sphinx takes us back to the Eighteenth Dynasty during the reign of Pharaoh Amenhotep, the great-grandson of Thutmose III who succeeded the female Pharaoh Hatshepsut.

Amenhotep had many sons and daughters, but our protagonist is the king's favorite, Prince Thutmose (a different Thutmose from the first three before Hatshepsut). The prince was an athletic young man who had many skills. He was a great hunter and fighter, a charismatic speaker, an expert rider, a wildlife explorer, and excellent in the art of archery.

Despite his status as prince and being beloved by the pharaoh, Thutmose had a problem: all his siblings hated him. Every day, they plotted against the prince in a desperate bid to discourage the pharaoh from naming him the successor to the throne of Egypt. These ploys made Thutmose look unworthy and cruel, and they soon escalated to blatant attempts on his life. Yet no one seemed to notice. Not his father, the king, or his mother, Queen Tiaa.

The worried prince began to keep more to himself and stay away from the pharaoh. Instead, he added one more skill to his long list of abilities—the art of sneaking out of the palace in disguise. To pull this off as frequently as he desired, Prince Thutmose enlisted the assistance of a few trusted servants. He would slip away from the royal court many times to hunt gazelles and wild beasts in the desert. He also yearned for the picturesque view of the pyramids of Saqqara and Giza.

During festivities or sessions at the royal courts where the pharaoh required Thutmose's attendance, he would be around for a minute and gone the next.

One auspicious day, Egypt was in a festive mood for the grand celebration of the sun god Ra. The celebration was to be held in Heliopolis, and every servant in the palace was tasked with readying for the ceremony.

With everyone else distracted, Prince Thutmose saw the perfect chance to sneak out of the palace for another one of his hunting trips. He could not afford to get seen, so he selected two of his most trusted servants to go on the trip with him. At the crack of dawn, the prince and his servants took their secret exit and made their way to the desert on his chariot.

They toiled the entire morning but caught nothing. By afternoon, the infamous baking-hot Egyptian sun was lashing their bodies with its rays. Prince Thutmose and his men rode fast for the north and slowly approached the pyramids of Giza.

These pyramids had been built by the great pharaohs of the Fourth Dynasty (Khufu, Khafra, and Menkaure) over a thousand years before the prince was born. Thutmose was fascinated by the sight of them and yearned to move closer to say a prayer to Harmachis, whose spirit inhabited one of the sphinxes of Giza. In ancient Egypt, a sphinx was revered as the manifestation of Horus and the protector of royal tombs.

The Great Sphinx of Giza.
https://commons.wikimedia.org/wiki/File:DSC_0088_Sphinx01.JPG

Prince Thutmose ordered his servants to wait under the shade of the palm trees while he rode in his chariot toward the pyramids. As the sun shone brighter, the ginormous sphinxes sparkled, and Khafra's pyramid looked different from the others. The head of the sphinx was carved in the likeness of Harmachis, and it protruded from the sea of sand around it while the rest of the sphinx was buried under the sand.

Despising the intense heat, Prince Thutmose dropped to his knees and prayed to the sphinx head shaped like Harmachis. He laid out all his troubles about how his own brothers and sisters were after his life, and he asked for divine help.

Moments later, the prince noticed something rather spooky. The eyes of the sphinx he was praying to moved. He could not believe it, so he continued praying. The eyes of the sphinx were inanimate and made of stone. It had to be all in his head—until it was too obvious to ignore.

Suddenly, the earth began to quake around Thutmose, and the sands drifted violently as the sphinx came alive and tried in vain to wriggle out from the sand. Prince Thutmose was bedazzled by the sight and fell back as the mystic sphinx opened its mouth and spoke with a great voice:

"Look upon me, Thutmose, Prince of Egypt, and know that I am Harmachis your father—the father of all Pharaohs of the Upper and Lower Lands. It rests with you to become Pharaoh indeed and wear upon your head the Double Crown of South and North...

Thutmose, my face is turned towards you, my heart inclines to you to bring you good things, your spirit shall be wrapped in mine. But see how the sand has closed in around me on every side: it smothers me, it holds me down, it hides me from your eyes. Promise me that you will do all that a good son should do for his father; prove to me that you are indeed my son and will help me. Draw near to me, and I will be with you always, I will guide you and make you great."

After this came a blinding bright light that knocked Prince Thutmose unconscious. When his eyes reopened, the sphinx had returned to its former lifeless state, still stuck in the sand.

The sun was setting and casting its sepia rays on the sand from the reddened sky, which means that the prince had been out for many hours. Nonetheless, it was the most extraordinary event that Prince Thutmose had ever experienced, and he vowed to fulfill the wishes of Harmachis if he ever became the pharaoh of Egypt.

"Harmachis, my father! I call upon you and all the gods of Egypt to bear witness to my oath. If I become Pharaoh, the first act of my reign shall be to free this your image from the sand and build a shrine to you and set in it a stone telling in the sacred writing of Khem of your command and how I fulfilled it."

With this, Thutmose mounted his chariot and sped off to find his servants, who had become worried at his long departure. Together, they rode back to the palace in Memphis, with the prince invigorated by his encounter with the divine.

True to Harmachis's words, Thutmose was declared the successor by his father, Amenhotep. The efforts of his royal siblings to besmirch him before the pharaoh, the royal court, and the people of Egypt failed.

From around 1401 to around 1397 BCE, the prince ruled Egypt as King Thutmose IV, the eighth pharaoh of the Eighteenth Dynasty of ancient Egypt.

As pharaoh, Thutmose IV kept his promise to Harmachis. He had the sphinx of Khafre's pyramid dug out from the sand and built a shrine at its feet. The myth of the Prince and the Sphinx was documented in hieroglyphics, etched in a tablet made from red granite and attached to the sphinx.

This ancient tablet was found only two hundred years ago, and its author was none other than Pharaoh Thutmose himself.

Chapter 15– The Adventures of Sinuhe

You will recall the Prophecy of Neferti that spoke of an apocalypse and how the ascension of a vizier named Amenemhat to the Egyptian throne was the only way to avoid it.

Amenemhat indeed became the pharaoh who founded the Twelfth Dynasty of Egypt, but his reign was not entirely peaceful. For many decades, he was in danger of being overthrown, just as he had overthrown the pharaoh before him, Mentuhotep IV. The king's reign was plagued by civil war and unrest that continued even after he made his son, Prince Senusret, next in line for the throne.

Times were delicate in Egypt, and the king's court reeked of conspiracies and rebellions against the pharaoh.

Our story begins with Prince Senusret, who was away in the east, fighting off foreign invaders, the Temehu tribe of Libya. The prince and his army emerged victorious, and after a bout of celebration, they rode for Egypt with the spoils of war. Among his esteemed officials was a warrior named Sinuhe, a staunch supporter of Pharaoh Amenemhat. Midway to Egypt, the prince and his men were met by messengers from the king's palace.

No one knew what news they had brought, but Sinuhe had a premonition that it was about the king. To ascertain the truth, he eavesdropped on the prince's conversation with the messengers. Indeed, Pharaoh Amenemhat had been murdered in his sleep by one of the many men who sought to end his life, and the prince was to be made the new king in his stead.

The prince was aggrieved to hear of his father's assassination, but Sinuhe was more afraid than sorrowful. If the king of Egypt had been killed by rebels, then they would target all who had supported him next. Sinuhe was also afraid that the prince was in danger of being murdered. No doubt, his reign would be the same as his father's, if not worse.

A Quest of Survival

Sinuhe backed away from the prince's camp and took to his heels. He snuck out of the military encampment under cover of night and traveled along the Nile toward the city of Heliopolis. He arrived at the eastern border of Egypt and advanced to the narrow strip of land between the Mediterranean Sea and the Red Sea called the Isthmus of Suez. From there, he moved quickly to the Desert of Sinai, where his thirst got the better of him.

Sinuhe had never been so dehydrated in his life. His throat was parched, and he could quite literally "taste death" in the middle of his self-imposed exile. His hands were soon numb, along with his knees, yet he crawled on in desperation to stay alive.

Then, he encountered his first stroke of luck: a camp of Asian nomads.

Sinuhe passed out from exhaustion, comforted by some hope that he might be rescued by the nomads. After a long deep sleep, he woke up and found himself cleaned, treated, and fed with milk and water. As it turned out, the nomads were on commercial and cattle grazing business in the Nile Delta area of Egypt, so Sinuhe could not continue with them.

He headed for Syria and arrived at Byblos, the kingdom that had received the goddess Isis when she had come to rescue her husband, Osiris. Sinuhe spent a few nights in Byblos, but it was a land friendly to Egyptians. It was not his destination.

Eventually, he arrived at a kingdom called Retenu (also called Canaan) in Lebanon.

A New Home

The king of Retenu was Ammienshi, and despite the toll that Sinuhe's trip had taken on his appearance, the king could tell that he was an important man from Egypt.

He welcomed Sinuhe to Retenu and offered him a home among the other Egyptians who lived in the kingdom. During their conversation, King Ammienshi inquired into the reason why Sinuhe had come so far from his home. This might have been the king's way of measuring the manner of man that he was. Sinuhe responded by telling the king of Pharaoh Amenemhat's passing and that he had fled Egypt because he feared that a civil war would erupt.

King Ammienshi was aware of the old pharaoh's death and of the ascension of Prince Senusret I as the new king of Egypt. He assured Sinuhe that there had been no revolts against the new pharaoh's reign and sought Sinuhe's counsel on whether or not to support the new pharaoh.

Sinuhe responded by saying noble words about the new pharaoh and entreating King Ammienshi to be loyal. From this, King Ammienshi gathered that Sinuhe was a man of peace and would not pose any threats to his kingdom. Sinuhe was also a man of war, though, which means he could be useful in a military capacity.

So, King Ammienshi made Sinuhe a commander of his armies and consented to his marriage to his first daughter. This elevated Sinuhe's status in Retenu, and he was given an estate called Iaa, which had rich, fertile lands for crops and cattle to flourish.

In his capacity as an army commander and tribal chief, Sinuhe embarked on many military campaigns to protect Retenu from foreign invasions. His services pleased King Ammienshi so much that he decided to make Sinuhe the next king of Retenu.

The Duel of Champions

King Ammienshi's succession plan did not sit well with some of the nobles and commoners in Retenu. They thought the king had spent too many years overcompensating a foreigner for his services, and the throne of Retenu was where they would draw the line.

A wind of rebellion was rumored to soon sweep through the palace, and it was to be championed by an undisclosed war hero in Retenu. Unable to shake off his anxiety, King Ammienshi summoned Sinuhe for a private discussion. He asked if Sinuhe knew the man who was planning a rebellion. Sinuhe answered no, but that would soon change.

There was to be a duel between him and the man who wanted him dead. This duel was to happen in public and in the king's presence. The war hero would reveal himself and fight Sinuhe to determine who was greater.

On the day of the duel, the people of Retenu trooped to the venue of the fight, and many cheered for Sinuhe. They had no doubts about his skills in archery and combatant warfare, and he had all it took to conquer his challenger—until they found out that Sinuhe's opponent was a giant.

The arena fell silent, gasping in awe at the giant's menacing physique. He was armed with arrows, a gigantic battle-ax, and javelins.

Doubts crept into the hearts of some of Sinuhe's supporters, and they feared that this fight would be his last. The battle began in earnest, and as they had feared, the giant was not a walkover. He charged at Sinuhe with every weapon in his armory, and Sinuhe escaped every attack by a hair's breadth.

In the heat of battle, Sinuhe chose an opportune time to hurl a javelin at his opponent. The javelin pierced the giant's neck, and he sank to his knees before dropping dead with a thud.

Jubilation erupted in the arena after Sinuhe cut off his opponent's head, and the king was overjoyed that his successor had won the battle. News traveled throughout the kingdom about the duel, and Sinuhe's greatness was enlarged. It was unlike anything it had been before. He served King Ammienshi for many more years and became king after him.

<u>The Homecoming</u>

"Return to Egypt to look again upon the land where you were born and the palace where you served me so faithfully."

Sinuhe could not contain his happiness upon reading a letter from the king of Egypt. He had sent a letter to ask for forgiveness and to be allowed to visit Egypt at least one more time before he died. It had been many years since Sinuhe left Egypt, and he was not as young as he once was. In his old age, he yearned to go to Egypt and see what his homeland now looked like.

He had not anticipated an express invitation to live out the rest of his days in Egypt, but Pharaoh Senusret I had graciously offered. Sinuhe's self-imposed exile was over, and the dangers of the past were long behind him.

Sinuhe quickly transferred the rulership of Retenu to his oldest son and set off on a long journey back to Egypt. He was welcomed by the king and the royal family. Many of the king's courtiers could not recognize him.

Pharaoh Senusret I was thrilled to be reunited with an old friend. He bore no grudges and mentioned nothing of the past. Instead, he directed that Sinuhe change out of his desert clothes and be given fine linens to wear. He was to be groomed and fed well.

This story ends with Sinuhe living out the rest of his days as a beloved friend of the king. This long-lost fugitive had found his way back home.

PART THREE: GODS AND GODDESSES

Chapter 16– Amun-Ra

You will recall from the creation myths of ancient Egypt that in Heliopolis, the creator was Atum. Hermopolis, Memphis, and Thebes eventually named Amun as their chief creator god. Atum and Amun are the same; they are both aspects of Ra.

Typically, Amun was worshiped as the morning sun and Atum as the light of night, but things were slightly different in early Egyptian history.

In the Old Kingdom era of ancient Egypt, Amun-Ra was worshiped as two different gods. Amun was the creator deity who had formed the world from the nothingness of Nun and created humans to dwell on the earth. Ra was the sun god who rode through the sky in his barque of light by day and descended to the underworld to defeat the monstrous Apophis (Apep) at night.

In Theban tradition, Amun was only a partner to the female Amaunet and a member of the revered Ogdoad. Unlike Ra, Amun was a spirit form and could only be felt, not seen or touched. Ra was the visible sun and the earth's soldier against the darkness (Apophis or Apep).

Amun was not associated with Ra, the sun god, until the New Kingdom. This may have been a result of the unification of Upper and Lower Egypt and the shifting of the Egyptian capital from Memphis, where Ra was supreme, to Thebes, where Amun was prominent.

The sun god Ra was syncretized with the creator god Amun to become the powerful Amun-Ra. With this, the attributes of the spirit creator god and those of the sun god were fused into a single universal deity.

Amun-Ra: The Creator

In Egyptian mythology, Amun was not born. He emerged from the primordial waters of Nun as a divine, self-created being. He was the first to exist on Earth, and the creation of the world was initiated by him. Amun's first creation was that of *heka*, the magic with which he made the rest of the world. In some traditions, Heka was a god, but in most, he was magic itself, just like Amun-Ra was the sun itself.

Next, Amun created his first children, Shu and Tefnut, who went on to populate the earth with their offspring. After them, Amun created Ma'at, the order of the world. Ma'at, as a goddess, was said to be the daughter of Ra, as were the goddesses Hathor, Sekhmet, and Bastet, who were sisters.

The Eye of Ra is another important aspect of Amun-Ra as a creator god. It is the feminine aspect of Amun. In the creation myth of Heliopolis, the Eye of Ra was sent on a mission to find Shu and Tefnut when they left home. In time, the Eye of Ra became more than just a part of Amun's body. The goddess Sekhmet (or Hathor) was often called the Eye of Ra, the fearsome messenger of Amun-Ra who once destroyed the world as a punishment for the sins of mankind against their creator.

Creation is the first role attributed to Amun-Ra, and in the years that followed the primeval era, the influence of Amun-Ra would only broaden. You will find Amun-Ra, the creator god, depicted in ancient Egyptian texts as a falcon-headed god with a snake-rimmed sun disk on his head. He is also portrayed in creation myths as a scarab beetle named Khepri or a young boy believed to be Horus.

The Forms of Ra: Khepri, the Eye of Ra, and the falcon-headed god.
Credit: HarJIT. Derived from files from Jeff Dahl, Rawpixel, Finn Bjørklid, Jasmina El Bouanraoui and Karabo Poppy Moletsane., CC BY-SA 4.0 https://creativecommons.org/licenses/by-sa/4.0 via Wikimedia Commons;
https://commons.wikimedia.org/wiki/File:Khepri_Re_Hypocephalus_Scene.svg

Amun-Ra: The Sun God

The most popular depiction of Amun-Ra in Egyptian mythology was as the traveling sun god. When the foundations of the earth were laid and Ma'at took its course, the day was divided from the night, but that did not just happen suddenly.

Indeed, it took the eternal voyages of Amun-Ra to create the miracles of dawn and dusk. The sun god had a shiny boat (or barque) called Atet, and on it, he would course the sky in the daytime as the sun. When evening came, he would descend on the western horizon to the underworld (the Duat) for twelve hours, fighting demons, judging wicked souls, and reviving the needy. In the twelfth hour, the sun god's barque would rise in the east, and the sun would reappear.

In his depiction as a sun god, Amun-Ra was typically shown as a ram-headed god with the sun disk on. He would also have companions on his barque, notably Heka (in his form as a god), Sia, and Hu (gods who represented the divine Ennead). You can also find pictorials of more popular gods like Set and Hathor as being part of Amun-Ra's entourage.

Amun-Ra on his divine barque (Atet) in the underworld.
https://commons.wikimedia.org/wiki/File:Book_of_Gates_Barque_of_Ra.jpg

Despite Amun-Ra's supremacy in the Egyptian pantheon, his journeys were not smooth-sailing. Every day as he descended to the underworld, he would be challenged by an infernal enemy, Apophis (or Apep). Some mythological versions say that Apophis attacked the sun god while he was in the underworld, not when he was descending into it. In any case, Amu-Ra fought off this monster every day and defeated it.

At the gates of the underworld, Amun-Ra would be received by his good friend, Osiris, the god of the underworld. Some Egyptian traditions outrightly fuse Amun-Ra with Osiris, but more generally, they were separate deities. Together, they would condemn the wicked souls of the dead to the Egyptian version of hell and grant the good souls passage to paradise.

Amun-Ra: The Father and King

Long before the era of the pharaohs, the gods ruled the earth. According to the sacred *Book of the Heavenly Cow*, the first king of the earth was Ra. He had just completed his fine work of creation and was the king of mankind—that is, until they began to rebel against him.

In the events that followed, Ra retired to the sky and created the Field of Reeds, the Egyptian version of heaven, for his abode. He also founded Ma'at and commanded humankind to uphold it with their lives.

As the creator of all life and the first in divinity, all other gods and goddesses were descendants of Ra. Apart from the association of Amun and Ra, which led to the emergence of Amun-Ra, or Atum and Ra, which became Atum Ra, there were others. There was the fusion of Ra with Horus, the falcon-headed god. Some depictions of Amun-Ra are as a falcon-headed god. The relationship between the two gods began in creation when Horus was portrayed in some mythological accounts as an aspect of Amun. The syncretism between Amun-Ra and Horus was called Ra-Horakhty.

These associations and his role in creating other deities enthroned Amun-Ra as the father and king of all gods. Naturally, this extended to mortals. Pharaohs of the Fourth Dynasty of the Old Kingdom called themselves the "sons of Ra." Thenceforth, the kings of Egypt became associated with Ra as his sons and divine representatives on Earth, for which they were revered by the people. They were also rumored to have built their pyramids in alignment with the sun as an act of worship.

The cult worship of Amun-Ra in dynastic Egypt began in Heliopolis. By the Second Dynasty, it had spread to the entire land, and the title of the sun god was widely assigned to Amun-Ra. He was the creator, the sun, and the god of the sun. In the Fifth Dynasty, the pharaohs began building temples of Ra, known as sun temples.

Userkaf, the founder of the Fifth Dynasty of ancient Egypt, was the first to commission a sun temple in the plains near Abu Gorab.

The sun temple was called Nekhen-Ra, meaning the "Fortress of Ra" or the "Stronghold of Ra," and its remains were unearthed in the early 1840s.

Six other sun temples would be built by Pharaoh Sahure, Pharaoh Neferirkare Kakai, Pharaoh Neferefre, Pharaoh Shepseskare, Pharaoh Nyuserre Ini, and Pharaoh Menkauthor Kaiu, all of them during the Fifth Dynasty.

The Opet Festival was the largest celebration of Amun in ancient Egypt. It peaked in the New Kingdom era around 1539 BCE in Thebes. It began on the fifteenth day in the first season of the year, Akhet (or the Season of the Inundation), and it was celebrated for eleven days during the reign of Pharaoh Thutmose III. It became twenty-four days when Ramesses III was on the throne, and soon after, it took as long as twenty-seven days.

The pharaoh was the most important figure in this celebration since he was the highest prophet of Amun in all the land. The Opet Festival was a time to legitimize his reign and status as the king of Egypt before his people. The pharaoh would be endued with the power of Amun, and as a sign of the god's blessing, the lands of Egypt would be fertile.

As part of the festival rites, a colorful procession of priests would bear the sacred statue of Amun in a gold-coated wooden barque from the temple in Karnak to the Luxor Temple. The people would flock to the streets to see the procession, anticipating the abundance of bread and wine that would soon follow. They would also anticipate their consultations with Amun through his priests for answers to life's problems.

While at Luxor, the pharaoh would enter the innermost room in the temple for the ritual transfer of power and rejuvenation. Afterward, the procession would return the statue to Karnak.

Amun-Ra had his own holiday in Egypt as its national deity. He appeared in every Egyptian myth and sacred book, and his sons and daughters, both mortal and immortal, lived their lives in his service.

The eminence of Amun-Ra remained uncontested throughout the Old and New Kingdom eras of ancient Egypt and even beyond. There was just no unseating the god who caused every new day to emerge and created everything in the world.

Chapter 17 – Isis, Osiris, and Horus

You will recall these three from the famous Myth of Osiris and how their influence stretched from the Old Kingdom to the eras that followed. Isis and Osiris were the first siblings. They were the children of the god Geb and goddess Nut (who were also siblings). They were also the great-grandchildren of the creator god Atum, at least according to the creation myth of Heliopolis, and they became the king and queen of Egypt.

Isis: Goddess of Healing and Magic

Praised as a major goddess in the Egyptian pantheon, Isis was first referenced in texts from the Old Kingdom as a main character in the famous Osiris myth. She fell in love with her brother Osiris from the womb and married him. Together, they ruled Egypt as king and queen.

Isis was born to Geb and Nut, along with her four (sometimes three) other siblings, who were all endowed with divine powers. In the myths of Osiris and that of Isis and the Seven Scorpions, Isis uses her magical powers to heal her husband and a dying child, respectively.

Her hieroglyphic name is often translated as "throne" or "Queen of the Throne," which is why she was regarded as the mother of all pharaohs. Isis is represented as a beautiful woman with black hair and cow horns on her head. She wears a red sheath dress and holds an ankh and a staff. Her symbols are the tyet (also known as the Knot or Girdle of Isis), the moon and solar disks, and sycamore trees. She is also portrayed as a majestic figure with outstretched wings or as a scorpion.

Isis, the goddess of healing.

The tyet is Isis's most prominent symbol, and it stands for life and well-being. The goddess Isis was not among the Egyptian gods and goddesses of creation, but her status grew over time. By the Roman era, the worship of Isis had reached its peak. She was honored as a queen, healer, mourner, mother, wife, and protector.

As the wife of Osiris, Isis showed tremendous support to her husband before he became the god of the underworld. When Set came after Osiris and killed him more than once, Isis never gave up on him. She rescued him and healed him with her magic powers, even when his body was mutilated. Isis soon became a model for the virtuous Egyptian woman. She was devoted and faithful to her husband, no matter the circumstance.

Isis's son, Horus, became associated with the pharaohs of Egypt, which made Isis become the queen mother of all the kings of Egypt. She became a significant divinity of protection, nourishment, and companionship for pharaohs from the Fifth Dynasty onward.

Besides her royal importance, the goddess Isis was worshiped as the protector of women and children. During her reign with Osiris, Isis was known to teach the women of Egypt how to master baking, weaving, and wine-making. This endeared Isis to the women, and they prayed to her for the preservation of their marriages and children. As shown in the myth of Isis and the Seven Scorpions, Isis had a soft spot for children. She also protected her own son Horus from the wrath of Set until he was old enough to avenge his father.

Another important aspect of Isis was her power of healing. She had brought Osiris back from the dead twice and healed Usert's young son in Egyptian mythology, earning her a prominent spot in the mystical matters of ancient Egypt. An ancient Egyptian book of spells tells the story of Isis healing the sun god from a snakebite wound in exchange for the knowledge of his "true secret name." This secret name of Ra is believed to carry immeasurable power, and Isis's possession of it was what made her the most powerful magical healer in the world.

In the myth of Osiris, Isis sorrowfully restored the king's broken body and helped him transition to the afterlife as the god of the underworld. This act made Isis a worshiped mourner and guide to the afterlife. During funerary rites, Isis would be invoked to make the deceased whole and preserve their soul in the afterlife.

Despite her fame across Egypt, it was not until the early to mid-300 BCE that the first temple of Isis was built. This happened during the reign of Pharaoh Nectanebo II, the last native ruler of Egypt. The Macedonian pharaohs who subsequently ruled Egypt carried on the legacy, erecting more structures for the worship of Isis throughout the land.

This made the cult of Isis, which had existed as early as the Fifth Dynasty, spread throughout the Mediterranean. Foreign sailors began worshiping Isis as their protector at sea, and her fame soon reached the shores of Rome, Greece, and other parts of Asia Minor. Travelers and merchants who joined the cult of Isis spread her worship in the cities and kingdoms of the Middle East, including Iran.

It had taken a long time for Isis to be independently worshiped within and outside Egypt and Nubia, but attributes of her care, empathy, and compassion soon attracted men, women, and children in the thousands to kneel at her feet.

<u>Osiris: The God of the Underworld</u>

When Osiris was born to his parents, Geb and Nut, he was predestined for greatness. Not only was he the firstborn and the heir to the throne of predynastic Egypt, but an epic clash with his brother would change the course of his life for all eternity.

The name Osiris has a rich debated etymology. While it is commonly agreed that the name "Osiris" is the Latin translation of the Egyptian name Asar, there are many meanings of the name itself, including "Seat of the eye (of Ra)," "the Mighty One," "the Beautiful One," and "the Created One."

You will find depictions of Osiris as a green-skinned man (like his father Geb) with a beard. He wears a long ostrich-feathered crown called the Atef and holds the royal crook and flail. Instead of a royal robe, his lower torso is wrapped like a mummy. In a few depictions, he is portrayed as having black skin instead of green, representing the fertile marshes of the Nile River.

Osiris was the god of life and the god of death. He was also the god of the afterlife since he was the judge of the dead, and he was the god of resurrection. These rather contrasting aspects allude to his journey as an earthly king and how it was renavigated to a reign of the underworld.

It's all in the legendary myth of Osiris.

During his reign in Egypt, Osiris was loved by his people for bringing peace and prosperity to the kingdom. As the god of fertility and agriculture, he taught his people how to cultivate the land and harvest food for their survival. With his wife and sister Isis, Osiris ruled Egypt with unmatched wisdom, much to the envy of his brother Set, who eventually murdered him twice.

After being raised from the dead by his wife, Osiris assumed his throne in the underworld as the judge of the dead. His death and resurrection were the dawn of a new era of worship, one that would transcend predynastic Egypt.

In line with his contrasting roles as an earthly king and the king of the underworld, Osiris is portrayed as both a kind, generous god and a dreadful deity who commanded demons of the underworld. He also had the powers to decide whether a soul would live on in the afterlife or be destroyed.

As an important figure in the afterlife, Osiris's worship spanned from around 6000 BCE to the Ptolemaic Dynasty (323 BCE–30 BCE). Annual festivals to commemorate his death and resurrection were held, and a city in Upper Egypt called Abydos became the center of the cult of Osiris.

During the festivities, the people would perform plays, telling the story of Osiris's murder and dismemberment, how Isis revived him and helped him transition to the afterlife, and the revenge of Horus. They would also build ridges on their farms called "Osiris Beds" and planted seeds of grain. The germination of these seeds was symbolic of the resurrection of Osiris, and it was heralded with rejoicing. Reliefs of this festival were carved on the tomb walls of Pharaoh Tutankhamun.

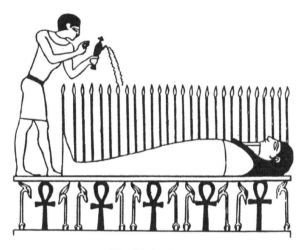

The "Osiris Bed."
https://commons.wikimedia.org/wiki/File:Osiris_Philae.jpg

By the Twelfth Dynasty, a five-day funeral ritual was held every year in Abydos, the worship center of Osiris. The events for each day were outlined on the Ikhernofret Stela, a scared stone slab in Osiris's temple. On the first day was a procession led by the god Wepwawet, the Opener of Ways. At this time, the people would perform a battle play where Osiris would triumph over his enemies. The second day was the Great Procession of Osiris. A statue of Osiris (representing his body) would be moved from the temple to his tomb in a boat. On the third day, the people would mourn the death of Osiris, and on the fourth day, the people would pray while funeral rites were performed. On the fifth day, the people of Egypt would celebrate the rebirth of Osiris at dawn and move the statue back to the temple in a celebratory style. This represented Osiris becoming ruler of the underworld and restoring Ma'at.

The Greek author Plutarch makes a different observation of the festivals of Osiris. He describes them as being gloomier and solemn, often restricted to the temple premises. He also tells of rituals of clay performed by the priests of Osiris. It involved mixing fertile soil with water in small golden coffers and molding crescent-shaped figures representing Osiris and Isis. Other accounts describe the baking of divine wheat bread and cakes from wheat grain grown in the temples of Osiris.

The ancient Egyptians believed that after death, every person qualified for the afterlife would be welcomed by Osiris. If not, a soul was damned to be devoured by the demon Ammit or cast into a fiery lake.

Osiris retained influence in the religious realms of ancient Egypt well into the Hellenistic Period (c. 323 BCE). This era fused Osiris with a Greek god named Serapis, and temples were constructed for their cults in Memphis and Philae.

Horus: God of the Sky

You may have seen pictures or depictions of a falcon-headed god from ancient Egypt. His name is Horus, and he was the son of the god Osiris and the goddess Isis. Not only was Horus a member of the beloved trinity of ancient Egypt, but he was also worshiped as the "Pharaoh of All Pharaohs."

Horus had an unusual childhood. He had been born to a mother who was on the run from a man who had killed his father and snatched his birthright. This shaped the nature of Horus's upbringing. He lived out his growing years in the swamps of the Nile Delta, hiding from his uncle. This is why many Ptolemaic figurines of Horus as a child are a young boy with a finger to his lips, indicative of silence. Under the protection of his mother,

Horus was trained in the art of magic, and his father, who had transitioned to the underworld, taught him the art of warfare.

The man who had disrupted his family was none other than his uncle Set, and it was Horus's destiny to destroy Set and save Egypt from a tumultuous reign. After years of battle against Set, Horus was victorious, and he reclaimed the throne of Egypt. Thereafter, the fame of Horus spread, and he made worshipers of many men and women throughout the land and in the generations to come.

The symbol of Horus is a falcon, and the Eye of Horus is believed to signify good health, healing, and protection. The Eye of Horus originates from a version of his conflict with Set, where Horus's eye was gouged out in the heat of battle. Horus's eye healed after the encounter, and he offered it to his father, Osiris, as a keepsake for the afterlife. Some ancient Egyptian traditions used the Eye of Horus and the Eye of Ra interchangeably since Horus was the offspring of the sun god.

Horus coming out of a lotus flower as the son of Ra.
Unknown author, CC0, via Wikimedia Commons;
https://commons.wikimedia.org/wiki/File:The_Sacred_Books_and_Early_Literature_of_the_East,_vo
l._2,_pg._272-273,_Horus.jpg

Horus was worshiped as the sky god, whose right eye was the sun and the left was the moon. He was also the falcon that soared in the sky, representing his status as "he who is above" or his kingship. This explains why Horus was associated with kingship, and all the pharaohs of dynastic Egypt proudly called themselves the descendants of Horus. They associated with him while they were alive, and in death, they were associated with Osiris.

Cults of Horus emerged in Edfu and Nekhen, the capital of Upper Egypt in predynastic Egypt. His temples were beautiful edifices with courtyards, lakes, and gardens. While only the priests could enter the innermost rooms that housed the statues of Horus, people from all over Egypt flocked to the temples to offer prayers, give and receive alms, and receive interpretations of dreams and signs.

The Festival of Victory was the most important celebration dedicated to Horus. It was a colorful event that was held in the month of *Meshir*, the second month in the Season of Emergence (the sixth month in the ancient Egyptian calendar). The people would converge in Horus's temple at Edfu and begin the festivities with a drama depicting Horus's triumph over his evil uncle Set. The pharaoh would play the part of Horus, and he would wrestle a hippopotamus, which represented Set.

If the pharaoh killed the hippopotamus, he would be respected by the people as the legitimate owner of the throne. If the king could not attend the festival in person, he could assign a priest to fill the role. It was important to put on a delightful show and display the power of Horus and his supremacy over Set.

The name "Horus" is arguably the name of the fifth son of Geb and Nut. This variation of Horus is known as Horus the Elder by those traditions that believe in his existence. Horus the Elder was the brother of Osiris, Isis, Set, and Nephthys. Other ancient Egyptian traditions name Hathor as the mother of Horus the Elder and further assert that he was the falcon god and the "Distant One."

He was a messenger from Ra to guide humans and comfort them until he transformed into the child of Osiris and Isis as Horus the Younger.

In Graeco-Roman Egypt, Horus became the equivalent of the Greek god Apollo, and Edfu, the city of Horus, was renamed Apollinopolis (the city of Apollo).

Chapter 18 – Set and Nephthys

Just like Osiris and Isis, the god of chaos Set and the goddess of death Nephthys were siblings who got married. This couple had vital roles in the Osiris myth, and in the end, they turned out to be a most unlikely pair. Were they ever in love? What happened to their marriage in the course of events involving their other siblings? What was their place in the Egyptian pantheon?

You are about to find out.

<u>Set: The God of Chaos</u>

Everything there is to know about this god from ancient Egypt is in the name. Every time there was a storm or a violent earthquake, the people of ancient Egypt would whisper to one another that it was Set at work. He represented everything foreign or disruptive to order, and he was the villain in nearly every story he was a part of.

Set, god of chaos.

Set was born to Geb and Nut, along with three (or four) others, and the myths agree that he had been a troublemaker from birth. He was even said to have had torn out of his mother's womb! Geb and Nut must have suspected that their new son would do great yet terrible things.

His childhood was set in predynastic Egypt, and one day, his parents announced Osiris as the crown prince of Egypt. Since Osiris was the firstborn, he was the first in line, with Set behind him. This made Set envious, but there was little to be done at the time. It was the natural order anyway, and their father Geb was going to be around for a while.

It was not long enough after that Geb abdicated the throne of Egypt and gave it to Osiris. The young king had many bright ideas to make the land prosper under his reign, and there was Set, who was unable to quell his growing bitterness and jealousy. While Osiris took Isis for his wife, Set asked for the hand of Nephthys.

With this, Set and Nephthys were married, but little is known about their love story or if it even existed. On the contrary, the union of Set and Nephthys has been described as loveless and unhappy, while that of Osiris and Isis flourished. This did not help Set feel any more love toward his brother, who was now the king. From the shadows, Set watched his older brother transform Egypt and bring the people knowledge of agriculture, arts, and civility. The queen was also loved by the people for teaching the women the art of weaving, baking, and making wine.

Through it all, Set desired the throne, and it grew increasingly difficult to turn the hearts of the people against his brother. Eventually, he managed to form a small group of traitors, but their collective influence was barely enough to oust Osiris.

As the years went by, Set wallowed in his desperation to disrupt the succession order of Egypt.

It must have been a long day of plotting against Osiris and failing woefully. Set returned home to more enraging news. Osiris had slept with his wife Nephthys, and the young Anubis, whom Set had taken for his own son, was actually Osiris's son.

The news that he had been tricked by the king pushed Set further into the hot depths of his anger and hatred. Set stormed to the palace and confronted the king about the scandal with his wife. Osiris was shocked to hear about Anubis, but he had an explanation about the night with Nephthys. Nephthys had actually tricked the king into sleeping with her by disguising herself as Queen Isis that night. Osiris was regretful about the incident and apologized to Set.

Set took the king's words with a grain of salt. Now, he had all the more reason to hate Osiris, and as it stood, killing the king was the only way he could get the throne. After all, Queen Isis had yet to give birth to an heir.

Upon returning home, Set found Anubis waiting to welcome him. Everything about the boy reminded him of Osiris and Nephthys. It reminded him of treachery. That night, Set rejected Anubis and had him exiled from his sight. He would no longer treat Anubis as his son again. It was Set's first real act as the god of chaos and violence.

Next, he conjured up another evil scheme to get rid of the king, and for the first time, Set achieved his aim. He had Osiris trapped in a coffin and submerged the coffin in the Nile River. He also took his followers and invaded the palace of Egypt, forcing Queen Isis to flee for her life.

Set took the crown of Egypt and put it on his head. His reign was marked with mercilessness and terror, and the once peaceful and prosperous Egypt became a warzone. Set relished every moment of it. He was nothing like his brother, and he cared little for the love or adoration of the people when they could fear and tremble before him instead.

King Set took on as many concubines as he could since Queen Nephthys had betrayed him, and he enjoyed his dark reign for some time. Except, one day, bad news came knocking.

Isis had somehow found her husband. She had brought him back to life, and she was pregnant with an heir! Set was maddened by what was a twofold disaster, and he could not spare a moment of inaction. He set off immediately to search for his brother and found him recovering around the marshes of the Nile. Set murdered Osiris again, and this time, he was going to make it impossible for Osiris to recover.

He dismembered Osiris's corpse into fourteen pieces and buried each part far away from the other. He also found Isis and had her imprisoned to await the same fate that had befallen her husband.

Little did Set know that he had run out of luck.

Before he could harm Isis, she escaped from captivity and continued the search for her husband's body parts. Worse still, Isis was being helped by Set's wife, Nephthys, and Anubis, whom Set had disowned.

With the birth of Horus, Osiris's son, Set could feel the end of his reign lurking, but he would do everything to prevent it, even if it meant killing his nephew.

The story of Set is not complete without his epic battle with his nephew Horus. It was the most significant battle in predynastic Egypt, and it was indeed one for the ages. You know the background, but the progression of the war, as described in an ancient myth titled "The Contendings of Horus and Set," gives more gory details.

It all began with Horus and Set embarking on extreme tasks for competition. The prize was the throne of Egypt, so both Horus and Set were ruthless in their endeavors. At the end of every mission, none was willing to concede to the other. Set was the god of chaos, and brute strength was one of his abilities. Horus was his equal, having been trained by his father, Osiris, who had become king of the underworld after being murdered the second time. Horus was also a master sorcerer. He learned these skills from his mother, Isis.

Their competition soon escalated to open assaults and destructive battles, which provoked concern from the other gods and goddesses of ancient Egypt. This led to a congress presided over by the Ennead (nine gods) of Heliopolis to determine the rightful owner of the throne of Egypt. In some accounts, the council was unable to reach a consensus, and the rift between Horus and Set dragged on painfully for eighty years. Horus and Set tore away at each other, and Set used every trick he had in his evil book, including mutilating Horus's eyes and attempting to defile him sexually. Horus had his eyes restored, and in some accounts, Horus caught Set's semen in his hands and tore off Set's testicles for revenge.

In the end, Horus emerged victorious, while Set took a shameful exit from the throne of Egypt. But was this the end of the road for Set?

With Set's villainous role in Egyptian mythology, especially in the stories of Osiris and Horus, you would expect that Set was treated similarly to Apophis (or Apep), the hated evil serpent who challenged the sun god Ra.

Despite his dark nature, Set had a surprisingly positive side to him. He was part of the entourage who traveled with Ra to and from the underworld every day. This epic twist created a place in the hearts of the people, and they worshiped Set. Some historians even argue that Set was a thoroughly misrepresented god and that he may not have been so evil after all.

As a glimpse into the good side of the god of chaos, we have the barque of Ra: the divine boat that ferries through the sky in the daytime and descends to the underworld at night. It also doubles as a warship for the sun god's encounter with the all-dreadful Apophis.

Set was almost always on this barque because no other god could fill the shoes of the "Protector of Ra." He was also known to slay Apophis on many occasions and rescue the sun god whenever he got hypnotized by the serpent. Apophis found a fierce opponent in Set, as they were both masters of trickery and shared a frightful thirst to win battles.

Set fighting Apophis to protect the sun god Ra.
https://commons.wikimedia.org/wiki/File:Set_speared_Apep.jpg

As a warrior and defender, Set was also believed to strengthen pilgrims on their journey to the afterlife. As it turned out, Set worked with Horus to guide the souls of the deceased into the afterlife, which is yet another thoroughly ironic aspect of his being. You should know that chronologically, the positive aspect of Set came first. He was first revered as the "Protector of Ra" and, in some traditions, as the god of love. He was a hero-god.

The cult of Set and his temples in Avaris and Ombus was widely attended by the people of Upper Egypt. He was highly venerated and popularized by the Nineteenth Dynasty Pharaoh Seti I (who was named after Set) and his successor Ramesses II. They openly associated with Set as their father and protector. In his temples, only the priests of Set could be near his statues or enter the inner rooms. Others could only pray in the outer parts of the temple, and priests were designated to help the people with offerings, prayers, weddings, funerals, or consultations.

Not long after Ramesses II's reign, especially with the incursion of foreigners into Egypt, Set's reputation transformed radically. More emphasis shifted to his role in Osiris's death and his evil tenure as the king of Egypt, leading to the gradual demonization of a once-loved god.

Set became the god of foreigners, god of the desert, and god of chaos at the end of the New Kingdom. He became associated with aggressive foreigners from Asia Minor who invaded and enforced their rule by proxy on Egypt. Set's Greek equivalent was Typhon, a hideous evil beast who fought against Zeus for control of the universe but was defeated and locked away in Tartarus forever.

Fascinatingly, Set's demonization did not end the worship of him. Rather than hate him, the people of ancient Egypt prayed to Set to ward off evil, especially in the afterlife. As he had been a protector of Ra, they earnestly prayed for his protection.

Another perspective to this reaction was the Egyptians' belief in Ma'at. For order to exist and be appreciated, there had to be disorder. For peace to be valued, there had to be chaos. Set existed to balance the scale of harmony in the world; otherwise, life would have no meaning.

Symbolically, Set had many forms, possibly because of his contrasting nature. He is depicted as a muscular man with brown skin and the head of a composite animal in some documents and as a fork-tailed beast with red hair in others.

The god of chaos retained influence well beyond the era he was demonized in, and this distinguishes him from the league of villains in Egyptian mythology.

Nephthys: The Goddess of Death and Darkness

Beyond the myth of Osiris, the goddess Nephthys does not make much of an appearance. Nonetheless, she was one of the Ennead, and her actions, although seemingly insignificant from an outside view today, largely affected the course of events in her family and in Egyptian mythology and even history.

Nephthys was born to Geb and Nut. Like Set, she must have found herself ever in the shadows of her famous sister Isis. She could relate to how Set felt about Osiris, and that may have been the attraction. Her marriage to Set was not said to be happy, especially since she secretly wanted Osiris.

There is no telling if her desire for Osiris had anything to do with the fact that she wanted what Isis had or if it was all just lust. However, we know that Nephthys was set in her ways to make Osiris look her way. Nephthys knew that Osiris only had eyes for his queen, which means there was only one way to seduce him.

That night, Nephthys took on a foolproof disguise and appeared before Osiris in the exact likeness of his beloved queen. Osiris had no reason to suspect that it was Nephthys in disguise, so he slept with her. Nephthys's sinister plan succeeded. She returned home to Set, who had been too occupied with his endeavors to notice her absence.

In time, Nephthys realized that her actions had provided Set with the justification he sorely needed to harm King Osiris. Set also discovered that her son, Anubis, was formed after she slept with Osiris, and he cruelly expelled the boy from his household. This marked a turning point in the story of Nephthys, as her actions thenceforth reflected remorse for the damage she had caused.

After Set killed Osiris so brutally, Nephthys helped her sister Isis find the king's body parts. They searched for a long time, and they were assisted by Anubis. After the sisters found the parts, Nephthys stayed to help revive Osiris. She also stayed to help nurse young Horus after he was born. He would grow to bring her husband to his doom.

Very little is known about Nephthys as the queen of Egypt, perhaps because she was hardly ever in the palace. Set also had enough concubines to take Nephthys's place while she sought to atone for her actions against Osiris and Isis. Nephthys spent so much time with Isis that they became twin goddesses, closely associated with each other in divinity.

The name Nephthys is often translated to mean "Mistress of the Temple Enclosure" or "Lady of the House." The goddess is portrayed in paintings and sculptures as a young woman wearing a headdress shaped like a house with a basket atop it, yet she was not a model housewife or homemaker. The house stands for the temple and priesthood. Because of her service to Osiris, Isis, and Horus, Nephthys was honored as a divine helper of the weak and the dead in ancient Egypt.

An image of Nephthys.
https://commons.wikimedia.org/wiki/File:Nephthys2.png

As the nursing mother of Horus, Nephthys was adored as the nursing mother of all pharaohs. She was also their protector and the breather of fire upon their enemies. As the wife of Set, Nephthys's worship peaked at the same time as Set's. There were no significant temples of Nephthys until the Nineteenth Dynasty, which was when Ramesses II and his father made Set a more famous god. A temple of Nephthys was built in Sepermeru, Upper Egypt, close to the temple of Set. As the sister and comforter of Isis, Nephthys was honored in Abydos as a helper of the dead. She helped the dead transition to the afterlife, she mourned for the grieving, and she comforted women during childbirth.

Like Isis, Nephthys possessed magical healing powers, and you would find ancient Egyptians wearing amulets of Nephthys in good faith that she would heal them of their illnesses. She was also invoked with Isis during embalmment and other preparatory funeral rites.

Finally, a twist to Nephthys's personality was her being a goddess who enjoyed offerings of beer during festivities. For one associated with death, mourning, and darkness, Nephthys's association with celebratory wine was ironic. It may have been another accessory to her compatibility with Set, whose reputation was just as dynamic.

Chapter 19 – Anubis and Thoth

The ancient Egyptian pantheon had well over a thousand gods and goddesses who were worshiped throughout the land. Their shrines, temples, and festivals in Egypt were world-famous, and the greatest legends of history were woven around these divine beings. From the primordial era to creation and after, the relationships that Egyptian gods and goddesses had with humans and with one another are the unique stories that shaped the history of ancient Egypt. Among these players were the gods Anubis, the patron of lost souls, and Thoth, the god of wisdom and magic.

This is their story.

<u>Anubis: The Patron of Lost Souls</u>

You can't talk about the gods of ancient Egypt without mentioning a certain god shaped as a man with the head of a jackal (or a dog). He was one of the most famous gods worshiped in ancient Egypt, and he stood at the gates of the afterlife to usher in souls. In the Pyramid Texts, he is depicted as one who stands with Osiris. He weighs the heart of every soul in the Hall of Truth to determine if they are worthy of the afterlife.

His name is Anubis.

A depiction of Anubis.
Unknown author, CC0, via Wikimedia Commons;
https://commons.wikimedia.org/wiki/File:The_Sacred_Books_and_Early_Literature_of_the_East,_vo
l._2,_pg._208-209,_Anubis.jpg

Before the popularization of the myth of Osiris, Anubis was believed to be the son of Ra, the sun god. Subsequently, Anubis's origin found roots in more interesting circumstances. He was the lovechild of Osiris and Nephthys, and he was raised as a son of Set until the latter discovered his true pedigree.

The name "Anubis" is Greek, and he was called "Anpu" before the Greeks came to Egypt. Anpu translated to "royal child" in ancient Egyptian, and this may have been in deference to Anubis's status as the son of a king.

Osiris's myth provides a glimpse into what could have been Anubis's childhood. Born to a father who was ever scheming against the king of Egypt and a mother who was either still obsessed with seducing the king of Egypt or regretting her actions, Anubis's childhood might have been lonely.

Ultimately, he was discarded without hesitation by Set, and Anubis left what he once called home. The Greek author Plutarch narrates that Anubis was abandoned by his mother Nephthys as a helpless infant and left without a parent until a certain goddess adopted him.

Whether Anubis was adopted as a helpless infant or a much older child, he became the son of Isis, who was on the run from Set. Many versions of the myth of Osiris cite Anubis as the one who saved Isis from prison after Set captured her. With his mother, Nephthys, he helped Isis assemble the dismembered body parts of Osiris. This action warmed the hearts of the ancient people of Egypt, and they saw Anubis as a protector, guide, and helper. And his roles in the afterlife were not far off from that.

First, Anubis was the "Embalmer-in-Chief" of ancient Egypt. In fact, he was credited with being the first to ever embalm a corpse in the history of Egypt. The corpse was that of Osiris after he had been killed by Set. As the inventor of this sacred Egyptian practice of preparing the dead for their new lives in the underworld, Anubis was commonly featured in funerary art. During mummification, one of the priests would wear a wooden wolf mask to physically represent Anubis while saying prayers for a successful preparation process.

Anubis was also the "Guardian of the Scales." After Osiris's descent to the afterlife and assumption of the throne as the king of the underworld (the Duat), he had much to do. Not every mortal was righteous enough to pass on to the afterlife. Some were to be condemned to hell as prey of Ammit. To determine the fate of each man, tests had to be done, and Anubis was commissioned with this process.

Each mortal's heart would be weighed on a scale in the Hall of Truth. On one side of the scale would be an ostrich feather, which signified Ma'at, order and truth. If the heart weighed lighter than the feather, the soul would be ushered into the heavenly afterlife, but if the heart weighed heavier than the feather, the soul would be condemned to Ammit's belly or an eternal lake of fire.

Man and woman, young and old, noble and commoner, no one was exempt from this trial. The gates of the afterlife were guarded righteously by Anubis, and only the light-hearted could gain entry.

Anubis was also called the "Protector of the Graves." It was a tradition in ancient Egypt to bury the dead on the western bank of the Nile River since it was seen as the gateway to the underworld. Anubis, being the "Foremost of the Westerners," was in charge of keeping the souls buried on the western bank safe, just as he had protected Osiris's body from Set once. In this legend, Set transformed into a vicious leopard to assault Osiris's corpse, but he was repelled and skinned by Anubis with a hot iron rod.

In deference to Anubis's heroic act, the priests of ancient Egypt would wear leopard skins when preparing a corpse. They would also send off the deceased with prayers to Anubis to guide them to the afterlife, which brings us to another one of Anubis's sacred duties; he was the patron of lost souls.

Whenever a person died in ancient Egypt, it was believed that unless they were guided into the afterlife, they could be lost forever. As another one of his many titles, Anubis was venerated as the "Master of the Secrets," for only he knew the road to the afterlife and what lay at its gates and beyond. In ancient royal tombs, depictions of Anubis leading the deceased mortal by the hand into the Hall of Truth were popular.

Anubis's sacred duties were a part of every crucial step into the afterlife. Anubis protected the dead, led them to judgment, administered their judgment, and welcomed them to the afterlife. He was an incredibly important deity. A few ancient traditions posit that he had been the first ruler of the underworld, but he became Osiris's righthand man when he took the throne. Considering the times when Anubis was born and his journey with Isis, the plausibility of this account remains widely debated.

Symbolically, Anubis was the black jackal god. The color black represented the discoloration of a corpse after being cleaned with a chemical called natron during mummification. Black also symbolized the color of the shores of the Nile River, as well as aspects of life, death, and rebirth in the afterlife—things that were all associated with the god Anubis.

Anubis was known to hate injustice and troublemakers, which is possibly one of the reasons he soon became an enemy of the god of chaos, Set. While he did not take center stage in any of the popular ancient Egyptian myths, Anubis's fame stretched from predynastic Egypt well into the era of Graeco-Roman Egypt. The Greeks compared him to their god Hermes, and as fellow believers in the concept of the afterlife, the Greeks shared reverence for Anubis. He was worshiped throughout the land, and many shrines were built in his name.

Cynopolis, an ancient city in Upper Egypt, was home to the esteemed cult of Anubis, and the cult had a vast followership. Every man and woman was keen on the preservation of their souls and a smooth transition to the afterlife. What better way to be assured of a place in eternity than worshiping the one who stood at the gates of the underworld and knew all its secrets?

Thoth: The God of Wisdom, Magic, and the Moon

Many gods and goddesses in ancient Egyptian mythology were in charge of things that were mostly spiritual and sacred, but this ibis-headed god who comes to us from the city of Hermopolis had more intellectual associations.

He was the god and inventor of writing, the one who created the many languages in the world. He was the righthand man of Ra, the arbiter of the gods, and the chief of the famous cosmological Ogdoad of Hermopolis. He was Thoth.

You will find illustrations of Thoth as a man with the head of an ibis or occasionally a baboon. Like many other gods, including

Anubis, Thoth is portrayed as holding an ankh, also known as the "key of life," as it symbolizes the immortality of the gods. Thoth is also commonly shown as wearing a royal crown or headdress, demonstrating his association with the god Shu, the son of Ra.

Thoth, the god of wisdom.
FDRMRZUSA, CC BY-SA 4.0 https://creativecommons.org/licenses/by-sa/4.0 via Wikimedia Commons; https://commons.wikimedia.org/wiki/File:Thoth_mirror.svg

In the creation myth of Hermopolis, Thoth is the self-begotten creator of the world order or Ma'at. In other accounts, he is the husband of the goddess Ma'at, who, with Anubis, weighed the hearts of souls against Ma'at and recorded the results. Thoth's association with Ma'at is the foundation of his existence as the god of wisdom.

In early Egyptian mythology, Thoth went from being the head of the Ogdoad of Hermopolis to being part of the sun god Ra's barque entourage. He would counsel the sun god and keep journals of their voyage. Thoth was believed to be the source of hieroglyphics, and he became the "Lord of the Scribes" and the partner of Seshat, the Egyptian goddess of writing, wisdom, and knowledge.

Thoth's intellect created other diverse forms of human knowledge, such as law, science, and the art of worship. He was a god of perfection and diplomacy who could never make mistakes in his judgment. This made him a confidant of Ra, as illustrated in the Hermopolitan myth of "Thoth and the Distant Goddess."

This myth began with a dispute between Ra and his daughter. This dispute was long, and eventually, Ra's daughter stormed out of his sight and went far away from him into the deserts. In time, Ra became concerned that his daughter had been away for too long and sent many messengers to bring her back. The most famous eventuality of this was that the sun god sent his eye, the Eye of Ra, to find his daughter and bring her back home, which was a success.

In another account, however, things were not so simple. Ra's daughter was too powerful to be brought home. Ra needed an intervention, and that was when he thought of Thoth. No other god was wise enough to bring home the Distant Goddess. He summoned Thoth and charged him with the task. In the end, Thoth returned with Ra's daughter, and as a reward, he was given a wife named Nehemtawy.

Another one of Thoth's golden achievements was what led to his becoming the god of the moon. Back in predynastic Egypt, the average year had only 360 days. The sky goddess Nut was pregnant from the actions of her brother and lover Geb, and their father, Shu, was not the only one who was unhappy about it. Her grandfather Ra was just as furious, and with his divine power, he cursed Nut so that she would not give birth on any day of the year.

It was a harsh punishment, and Nut was distraught until Thoth learned of her plight and came to her rescue. He visited Iah, the god of the moon (or the moon itself), and requested Iah to give him some moonlight time. The moon god was intrigued by Thoth's request, but such a favor could not be granted so easily. So, the two gods made a gamble, and Thoth won, earning him the prize of moonlight time. Iah let Thoth have the moonlight time he needed, which was about five days.

With this, Thoth added five days to the year, allowing Nut to bypass Ra's punishment and give birth to her children, one on each day: Osiris, Isis, Set, Nephthys (and Horus in some accounts). Ra heard of Thoth's wisdom and was more impressed than enraged. This is believed to be the beginning of Thoth's relationship with the sun god. Ra gave Thoth an elevated place on his sacred barque and sought his counsel to defeat the evil Apophis (Apep).

In the myth of Osiris, Thoth played the role of a counselor and mediator. He was the one who suggested to Isis to find her husband's body parts and told her the magic words to say to bring him back to life. He also guided Anubis when he helped Isis escape from Set's captivity.

When the war between Horus and Set broke out, Thoth took on the role of the arbitrator, adding "God of Equilibrium' to his many titles.

Thoth was the one who ensured that each battle was fair, and he guided Horus on how to heal his eye when it was ripped out by Set in the heat of battle. "The Contendings of Horus and Set" negates the existence of Thoth before this war. Instead, Thoth was born from Set's forehead after Set's accidental contact with Horus's semen. He became a mediator thenceforth.

The influence of Thoth in ancient Egypt was propagated by the authors, librarians, and scholars of the time, who doubled as his priests. They honored him as the father of writing and the inventor of words. They also used the ibis, the symbol of Thoth, as their emblem and were versed in magic spells in the name of Thoth. The cult of Thoth soon emerged from the city of Hermopolis, and his worship had spread throughout the land by the end of the New Kingdom. During the festivals of Thoth, thousands of ibises and baboons would be mummified and sold to worshipers to give as offerings to Thoth. An excavation of the ancient sites around these worship centers, notably in Hermopolis, revealed a large number of these mummified animals.

"Thutmose," meaning "born of Thoth" or "Thoth is born," was the name of five pharaohs, three known viziers, and a famous sculptor in ancient Egypt. The wide association with Thoth by the nobility shows his influence, which held its momentum from predynastic Egypt until the emergence of early Christianity in Roman Egypt.

Being lovers of all things artsy and civilized, it was no wonder that the Greeks highly revered Thoth. Like Anubis, he was equated with Hermes and syncretized to become Hermes Trismegistus in the Hellenistic era. Hermes Trismegistus represented a holy blend of spiritual and material wisdom, as personified by Thoth and Hermes, and he was believed to author many books, collectively called the *Corpus Hermetica*.

Finally, ancient Egypt's god of wisdom was a secretary in the afterlife who stood next to Osiris and Anubis in the Hall of Truth, keeping account of every heart weighed against the feather of Ma'at. Thoth was also famous among the souls in the afterlife as a hospitable host for those who sought rest at his residence, the Mansion of Thoth. He also granted protective spells against the demons that lurked in eternity.

Chapter 20 – Hathor and Bastet

Two other goddesses who enjoyed reverence and relevance in ancient Egypt were Hathor and Bastet. In the Metropolitan Museum in New York City, you can find a plaque of Hathor and Bastet on display.

This artifact is traced to the Eighteenth or Nineteenth Dynasty, sometime between the reign of Pharaoh Ahmose I and Pharaoh Ramesses I. The artifact portrays Hathor as a sistrum, a musical instrument from ancient Egypt, playing to a cat, a symbol of Bastet. These two goddesses were associated with the arts and joy in ancient Egypt, but there was a lot more to them.

<u>Hathor: The Mother of the Sky</u>

Hathor's origins are as multi-versioned and dynamic as her attributes, but every story establishes her connection with the sun god Ra. Before Isis became popular as the "Queen Mother of all Pharaohs," Hathor held that title. After all, she was the mother of the sun god himself or, in other accounts, his daughter or consort and companion on the divine barque. Alternately, she was seen as the mother of Horus who symbolized rebirth, rejuvenation, and beauty.

Her most popular title was the "Mother of the Sky," which ... been conferred on her because of her association with Ra. The ancient Egyptians believed that the sky was where the sun journeyed through each day and that the sky was where the sun was reborn at the break of every dawn. This translated to their belief in Hathor as the mother of Ra, who gave birth to the sun every day—a cosmic mother. "The Golden One" was in deference to Hathor's status as an important member of Ra's company on his divine barque. She was the reason that the sun shone so bright and gave the world resplendence.

The cow is Hathor's animal, and depictions of her are a woman with the head of a cow or wearing a headdress with crown horns protruding from it and a sun disk in the middle.

An image of Hathor.

In other representations, Hathor is a cow or a sistrum, a percussion instrument she used to rid the land of Egypt of misfortune and sadness. She was also represented as a sycamore tree whose milky sap alluded to life and fertility.

As an equal of the Greek goddess Aphrodite and the Roman goddess Venus, Hathor was revered as a goddess of beauty and love in ancient Egypt. She was popular among the women as a representation of spiritual and physical femininity and as a divine midwife. Her role in femininity often leads to Hathor being compared with Isis, the wife of Osiris, and Mut, the partner of the god Amun. These three shared similar aspects, but Isis represented a more conservative side of femininity: the model mother and wife. Mut represented a more assertive feminine aspect, as she was typically independent. Hathor was free-spirited, openly sexual, and fun-loving, and, as you are about to find out, Hathor's reputation wasn't always that of a happy and benevolent deity.

In ancient texts from the Middle Kingdom to the New Kingdom, Hathor was the feminine aspect of the Eye of Ra, which was seen as Ra's messenger and harbinger of doom. According to an ancient legend, the sun god grew displeased with the state of moral decadence in the world he had created. Humankind no longer worshiped him and blatantly rebelled against him. As a punishment, Ra sent his daughter, Hathor, to wreak destruction on humanity. For this, she transformed into Sekhmet, the lioness-headed goddess of war, and she destroyed the world as instructed.

As she ravaged the earth with her hot breath of fire, the other gods were worried about Sekhmet's surging bloodlust. They asked the sun god to show mercy and call Sekhmet back from her sinister mission. If she was not stopped, she would wipe out every human alive, and the world would be empty and meaningless again.

Ra saw reason and decided that he would stop Sekhmet, but she was too far gone in her destructive spiral. There was one other way to stop her. Ra instructed for a special kind of beer to be made for Sekhmet. It was made with extra alcohol and blended with red dye to give it the appearance of blood. Sekhmet received the beer and, mistaking it for blood, took several gulps of it all at once.

Moments later, she was overcome with dizziness and fell into a deep sleep. Three days after, Sekhmet woke up as Hathor, the kind and gracious goddess. She became popular since she was the opposite of what she had been as Sekhmet. The story ends here in many versions. However, a variation of this myth does not end with Sekhmet turning good just yet.

Instead, it provides a fascinating prequel to "Thoth and the Distant Goddess," in which Thoth is sent to bring a daughter of Ra back home. Legend tells that the daughter of Ra was actually Hathor (or Sekhmet). She had woken up from her deep sleep and realized that she had been tricked by Ra. Her wrath knew no bounds.

A heated argument ensued between father and daughter, and Hathor left home for a faraway land as a sign of rebellion against the sun god for his trickery. Unable to bring her home, Ra sought the services of Thoth, the god of wisdom. Only he was able to get the job done, but he had to convince Hathor 1,077 times before that happened. The daughter of Ra may have started on her path of becoming good after coming home.

"Goddess of Love" was another one of Hathor's titles, and it told of the sexual aspect of this goddess. Even the gods were not immune to erotic pleasure, and as a consort of Ra, Hathor is depicted to have stimulated the sun god sexually to lift his spirits on many occasions. In other depictions, she is a beautiful woman with gorgeous hair, with each lock representing irresistible charm. Hathor may also have appeared to mortal men as a naked, attractive woman.

Ancient Egypt was a center for the arts, music, and dancing—an integral feature of their religious festivities. Hathor relished the view of celebration, whether it be eating, drinking, singing, dancing, or the women looking their best and smelling exquisite. Hathor could not resist the fragrance of incense any more than she could resist a good drink of wine. Like Nephthys, Hathor would get drunk while hearing the sistrum play.

Musical instruments were the keynote in the worship of Hathor. Apart from her favorite, the sistrum, the people worshiped the goddess of joy by singing hymns and playing lutes, harps, and tambourines. Every year, the people of Egypt celebrated Hathor by bringing flowers and dancing all the way to her temple in Dendera.

Hathor was fun-loving and dangerously adventurous, but she was also the goddess of tourism and trade. She was believed to be ancient Egypt's border protector who ensured that every ship on the Nile and Egyptian ships on other rivers and seas were safe. If you recall in the myth of the Greek princess, the temple of Hathor was where Helen sought refuge, and it was located near the shores of Egypt. In the myth of "Thoth and the Distant Goddess," Hathor left home for a faraway place, possibly Libya or Nubia, and became famous in these lands.

Through ancient Egypt's foreign trade relations, Hathor's fame spread to Canaan, Punt, Syria, and parts of Sinai. At the time, the vast turquoise and malachite reserves in the Sinai Peninsula made it a mining hot spot. With the spread of Hathor's worship into Sinai, she became the "Lady of Turquoise" and "Lady of Malachite." Egyptian traders who traveled to these foreign lands returned home with exotic items, which they called Hathor's gifts to Egypt (or to the pharaoh), as many mining sites were worship grounds in honor of Hathor.

As you would expect, the goddess Hathor was not without a role in the afterlife. Funerary art and literature from the earliest times in Egyptian history describe Hathor's first visit to the afterlife as a stopover between Egypt and foreign lands.

The Duat was crowded as could be, and many souls needed guidance in the afterlife. Hathor offered a helping hand and manifested as Imentet, the goddess of the west. She then joined the league of gods and goddesses who participated in the transition of souls. As Imentet, Hathor cared for the souls of the dead by nourishing them with food and drink. This shows Hathor's motherly nature, as well as her attributes as a protector and guide.

Pharaoh Horemheb with the gods Hathor, Osiris, Horus, and Anubis.
Jean-Pierre Dalbéra, CC BY 2.0 https://creativecommons.org/licenses/by/2.0
via Wikimedia Commons
https://commons.wikimedia.org/wiki/File:La_tombe_de_Horemheb_(KV.57)_(Vall%C3%A9e_des_R
ois_Th%C3%A8bes_ouest)_-4.jpg

The myths of the doomed prince and the two brothers portray the Seven Hathors, another aspect of Hathor. They were the knowers of fate.

Bastet: The Goddess of Protection

Like Anubis, there is no misrecognizing the cat-headed goddess of ancient Egypt and her slender body. She often holds an ankh and a sistrum. Her name is Bastet (or just Bast), and she was the rave of Lower Egypt for a considerable length of time.

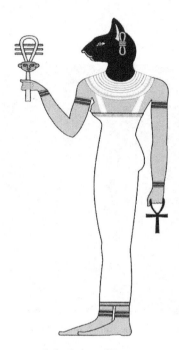

A depiction of Bastet.
Gunawan Kartapranata, CC BY-SA 3.0 https://creativecommons.org/licenses/by-sa/3.0 via Wikimedia Commons: https://commons.wikimedia.org/wiki/File:Bastet.svg

It is important to emphasize how much the ancient Egyptians adored cats; they practically worshiped them. The royal household of Egypt would dress up their cats in golden earrings, nose rings, and neckpieces. These cats would also eat with them at their tables. Among commoners, cats were not treated much differently. Even if they could not afford expensive ornaments, they did not take the creatures for granted. After all, cats protected the household by keeping destructive pests such as mice and snakes away. Excavations of the temple of Bastet revealed hundreds of mummified cats, and historians suggest that giving cats the same burial as humans may have been a thing in ancient Egypt.

The earliest origins of Bastet were as a lioness-headed goddess. She was believed to be the daughter of Ra and skilled in the art of warfare. She became associated with cats in the Twentieth Dynasty, which was in the New Kingdom. Her association with Ra meant an association with Hathor as Sekhmet, which is why Bastet and Sekhmet are described as sisters.

Like Sekhmet, Bastet manifested as the initially terrifying Eye of Ra but subsequently softened her reputation by becoming the scourge of Apophis (Apep) on the sun god's divine barque. Legend has it that at the behest of Ra, Bastet, in the form of a cat, would defeat Apophis by beheading the serpent with a sword in her paw.

Apart from Ra and Sekhmet, Bastet was associated with Isis for her protective nature. You will find many alabaster sculptures of Bastet with a litter of kittens at her feet. This alluded to her status in divinity as the goddess of fertility, pregnancy, and childbirth. Cats are known to be highly protective of their offspring, and this nature was conferred on Bastet following her transformation. She was revered as a mother and protector against sicknesses and misfortune. She was seen as being equal to the Greek goddess Artemis.

The worship of the cat goddess began in Bubastis, where her cult was established. Bubastis was a Nile Delta city in Lower Egypt that became the eighteenth regional capital of ancient Egypt. This brought the worship of Bastet more into the spotlight, spreading to Upper Egypt from Bubastis and Memphis. The Greek writer Herodotus in his work, the *Histories*, describes the mass transit of people from all over Egypt to Bubastis for the grand festivals in honor of Bastet:

"When the people are on their way to Bubastis, they go by river, a great number in every boat, men, and women together. Some of the women make a noise with rattles [sistrums], others play flutes all the way, while the rest of the women, and the men, sing and clap their hands...When they have reached Bubastis, they make a festival with great sacrifices, and more wine is drunk at this feast than in the whole year besides. It is customary for men and women [but not children] to assemble there to the number of seven hundred thousand, as the people of the place say."

The magnificence of Bastet's temple in Bubastis further spurred Herodotus to describe it. It was situated on an island, accessible via two routes from the Nile River. The temple was built in a central location in the city, so there was no missing its resplendent view. It had majestic stone carvings and was surrounded by tall grove trees that "reached to heaven."

The people would wear protective amulets that depicted cats, signifying Bastet's protection. They would also exchange gifts of kittens on New Year's Day. It was believed that these acts would rid the year of evil and herald prosperity.

Bastet did not have as many attributes as Sekhmet, and she was also not a part of the primordial Ennead like Isis. Yet, she remained an influential deity well into the Persian invasion of Egypt in the late 500s BCE and beyond. Roman Egypt also saw decades of her relevance, and for most of those years, the goddess of cats was an immense joy to the people.

PART FOUR: THE SACRED BOOKS

Chapter 21 – The Coffin Texts and the Book of the Dead

By now, you know all about the importance of life after death in ancient Egypt and how this belief shaped the lives of the people for many years. You also know that funerals in Egypt were not simple or rushed. Deliberate spiritual processes were undergone to seal the transition of the dead to the Duat in the hopes that they had followed Ma'at their whole life, or at least enough to qualify for paradise.

In Chapter 1, you read about the ancient sources that provided us with all the knowledge of Egyptian antiquity there is. A few names like the Pyramid Texts come to mind, but in this chapter, the spotlight is on two other important sources that came after the Pyramid Texts.

<u>Coffin Texts</u>

For a long time in the Old Kingdom, only pharaohs were buried with funerary art in their tombs. The walls of kings like Unas, Pepi I and Pepi II, and Menkaure I, and even queens like Neithhotep, Behenu, and Ankhesenpepi II had corpuses of texts carved into them to hasten the royal's journey to the Duat, which was at the time believed to be in the sky.

There was no book titled "Coffin Texts" in ancient Egypt. What exists as the Coffin Texts are compilations of texts recovered from multiple coffins during excavations by 19th-century archaeologists. These texts were translated from their originally written form to hieroglyphics by Dutch Egyptologist Adriaan de Buck, and they are valuable sources when studying ancient Egyptology.

Much of what made up the Coffin Texts were spells that were carefully etched into the inner part of the coffin before putting the corpse inside it. These spells currently number 1,185, and most make references to mythical stories from predynastic Egypt, such as Osiris's myth. This myth is the most recurring story in the Coffin Texts.

Before its popularization, the afterlife was perceived as the eternal home of the kings alone, as well as a few privileged queens. Old Kingdom nobles, scribes, and commoners did not believe that they could share such glorious eternity with their leader.

However, with the phenomenal discovery of Osiris's descent, not ascent, into the afterlife (or the Duat), the people realized that they had been wrong. The Duat was not in the sky or beyond their reach. Every person, king or not, who believed in Osiris and lived their lives in accordance with Ma'at could enter paradise. The cult of Osiris propagated this belief throughout the late Old Kingdom.

Consequently, from 2100 BCE, the Coffin Texts gradually replaced the Pyramid Texts, and the concept of the afterlife became far less exclusive. With this, non-royals could afford fairly elaborate funerals and all the materials required to make them so. Effigies, figurines, ceramics for burial vessels, precious metals, granite, and materials for mummification were no longer for pharaohs only. Production efforts were geared at making slightly inferior quality versions of these materials for commoners to use.

This impact on the spiritual and cultural outlook of ancient Egypt made Osiris's myth and its protagonist a most famous highlight of many Coffin Text spells.

"Ah Helpless One!

Ah Helpless One Asleep!

Ah Helpless One in this place

which you know not, yet I know it!

Behold, I have found you [lying] on your side

the great Listless One.

'Ah, Sister!' says Isis to Nephthys,

'This is our brother,

Come, let us lift up his head,

Come, let us [rejoin] his bones,

Come, let us reassemble his limbs,

Come, let us put an end to all his woe,

that, as far as we can help, he will weary no more.

May the moisture begin to mount for this spirit!

May the canals be filled through you!

May the names of the rivers be created through you!

Osiris, live!

Osiris, let the great Listless One arise!'"

This excerpt was a popular protective spell in many Coffin Texts. While it told of how Isis and Nephthys revived Osiris after he was killed by Set, it also invoked the two goddesses to protect the deceased on their journey to the afterlife.

Descriptions and invocations of guardian gods and goddesses were also found in the Coffin Texts. These were believed to help the deceased soul recognize guardians in the afterlife and submit to their protection. With demons, snares, and traps lurking at every stop, a soul needed divine help to navigate the Duat until they reached paradise. An unguarded soul was at risk of dying a second death or getting lost forever, so you can imagine that ancient Egyptians were finicky about the content in their coffins.

With the growing fame of Osiris as the judge of the underworld, the Coffin Texts provided the earliest known sources of events in the Duat, such as the judgment of the dead in the Hall of Truth. The most famous source from this era was the *Book of Two Ways*, which has an intricate map of the Duat and is, so far, the oldest illustrated book in history.

The author of the *Book of Two Ways* may never be known, but copies of the document were carved onto some ancient coffins from a village called Deir el-Bersha. No doubt, the people had copied this map from an original in the belief that the map would guide the deceased soul through the realms of the Duat. The oldest copy of this book was found in the tomb of a woman named Ankh, who was presumed to have lived during the Eleventh or Twelfth Dynasty.

In this book, there were two routes to paradise, which is why it is called the *Book of Two Ways*. The two routes were by the sea and land, which were separated by a fiery lake and hideous monsters. Both routes were riddled with perilous obstacles through which the soul must endure before appearing before Osiris.

As the most advanced version of the Coffin Texts, the *Book of Two Ways* would be replaced with the *Book of the Dead* in the Middle and New Kingdoms.

The *Book of The Dead*

The evolution of the Egyptian belief in the afterlife and its intricacies began with the Pyramid Texts, which dominated most of the Old Kingdom. Subsequently, the Coffin Texts, which drew on the Pyramid Texts but were more generally accessible, became more dominant. The highlight of the Coffin Texts was the *Book of the Dead*, which many Middle Kingdom Egyptians adapted to their funerary practices.

The emergence of the New Kingdom flagged a new stage in this evolution, and the *Book of the Dead* was the latest rage. Unlike the Coffin Texts, which were only drawn or carved on coffins, Twelfth Dynasty copies of the *Book of the Dead* could be written on papyrus and buried with the dead.

Like the Coffin Texts, there is no single *Book of the Dead*. Instead, there are compilations of many copies found in ancient tomb sites and coffins. A total of two hundred spells, hymns, and recitals were translated from their original hieroglyphic versions.

As the name implies, the *Book of the Dead* was written for the dead. It was a manual for overcoming dangers in the afterlife. The first spell was a prayer to Ra (or Atum) for the dead to successfully transition to the Duat. Also compiled in the *Book of the Dead* were spells to be recited by the deceased for the preservation of their bodies and protection from evil in the form of serpents like Apep:

"O you waxen one [Apep], who take by robbery and who live on the inert ones, I will not be inert for you, I will not be weak for you, your poison shall not enter my members, for my members are the member of Atum. If I am not weak for you, suffering from you shall not enter into these members of mine. I am Atum at the head of the Abyss, my protection is from the gods, the lords of eternity, I am He whose name is secret, more Holy of a throne than the Chaos-gods; I am among them, I have gone forth with Atum, I am one who's not examined, I am hale, I am hale!"

Some spells allowed the deceased to shapeshift into the forms of gods to fight against attackers. With one spell, for example, the deceased could transform into the sun god Ra to fight off savage crocodiles:

"Get back! Retreat! Get back, you dangerous one! Do not come against me, do not live by my magic...O you with a spine who would work your mouth against this magic of mine, no crocodile which lives by magic shall take it away."

There were also spells in the *Book of the Dead* that were meant to empower the dead to board the safest ferries in the underworld:

"O bringers of the ferry over this difficult sandbank

Bring me the ferry, tie for me the cords, in peace, in peace

Come, come, hasten, hasten, I have come to see my father Osiris."

The longest and most popular spell, Spell 125, described the judgment of souls in the Hall of Truth lucidly. It portrayed the jackal-headed god Anubis as the one who weighed the hearts of every man, with Thoth by his side and Osiris as the chief judge.

Left to right: A soul's heart being weighed by Anubis, recorded by Thoth, and then standing before Osiris, who is sitting on the throne.
https://commons.wikimedia.org/wiki/File:The_judgement_of_the_dead_in_the_presence_of_Osiris.jpg

The *Book of the Dead* was also a script containing the words that the deceased were expected to recite at every stage of their journey. An example was the "Declaration of Innocence" before the forty-two judges. Other aspects of the *Book of the Dead* indicated what each soul was to wear in the afterlife, such as a "heavenly white garment and sandals."

The *Book of the Dead* was commonly written by scribes who were well versed in spells. Unlike the Coffin Texts, which personified the deceased with Osiris, the *Book of the Dead* could be custom written for an individual or family. This would require the scribe to be familiar with the individual's identity, life story, physical features, personality, and pedigree. So, if a person was gravely ill and near death, they would request a scribe to draft a *Book of the Dead* for them.

Producing a *Book of the Dead* cost a fortune because of its importance in the afterlife. It is estimated to have cost up to half the annual wages of a laborer in ancient Egypt or a little over three ounces of silver. This made the *Book of the Dead* affordable mostly to the Egyptian aristocratic class and were often used more by men than women. Lower nobles who could afford secondhand papyrus and prefabricated versions owned a few copies. Scribes and priests could write for themselves, paying only for the materials to be used, not the workmanship.

Later in history, scribes began to write cheaper versions for the common folk. These versions had fewer spells and instructions and were written on far less quality papyrus. The commoners in this era took advantage of this, as it gave them a better chance at making it to paradise. Scribes made a fortune from this demographic for thousands of years, and consequently, there were many variations of the *Book of the Dead*. The more standard versions were found in royal tombs and burial chambers of bureaucrats, while the abridged versions were found in the coffins of commoners.

The highlights of the *Book of the Dead* are the journey of the dead in the Duat, the judgment of a soul, and spells for the protection of souls from a second death.

Chapter 22 – The Books of Caverns, Gates, and the Heavenly Cow

The importance of funerary art from ancient Egypt as a source of history cannot be overemphasized. Much of what is known about the Egyptian afterlife was described on the walls, ceilings, and roofs of ancient necropolises, coffins, and royal tombs.

You know all about the Pyramid Texts from the Old Kingdom, as well as the *Book of the Dead* from the New Kingdom.

One day in 1903, two archaeologists named Margaret Murray and Flinders Petrie discovered another form of funerary text on a corridor wall of an ancient temple of Osiris located in Osireion. This text was different from the Coffin Texts or the *Book of the Dead* in that it gave more gory details about what befell the souls condemned to the Egyptian hell in the Duat.

Incomplete versions of this text were found in the royal tombs of Pharaohs Ramesses IV, Ramesses VI, Ramesses VII, and Ramesses IX—they were all from the Ramesside era of the Twentieth Dynasty. There were also fragments of these texts in other non-royal tombs, totaling thirteen versions altogether. These texts were translated in the early to mid-1900s and compiled into a document titled the Book of Caverns.

The Book of Caverns

The complete versions of the Book of Caverns were found in the temple of Osiris and the grand tomb of a wealthy royal scribe from the Twenty-sixth Dynasty named Pediamenopet. The complete version has two parts; each part has three vertical sub-parts or sections, making a total of six sections.

The Book of Caverns tells the story of the sun god's journey in the underworld, the reward of saintly souls who pass the judgment, and the terrible plight of the souls who do not. The sun god's journey through the Egyptian "hell" happened every night, and the Book of Caverns illustrates every step of it with pictorials and texts.

In the first section of the Book of Caverns, the sun god is about to enter the Duat, standing at its gates.

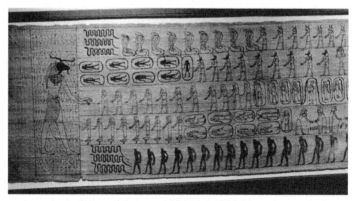

The first section of the Book of Caverns.
Tim Sneddon from Perth, AUSTRALIA, CC BY-SA 2.0 https://creativecommons.org/licenses/by-sa/2.0 via Wikimedia Commons;
https://commons.wikimedia.org/wiki/File:Extracts_from_the_Book_of_Caverns_(9174917894).jpg

Waiting to receive him in the Duat is Osiris, the god of the underworld and judge of the dead. The first section also has five sub-parts called "caverns." The first cavern above the sun god is guarded by three snakes. These snakes protect the bodies of saintly souls in the first and second caverns, where they rest for eternity.

The third cavern is where the sun god directly enters. Osiris sits there in two forms. The first form reaches out to the sun god, and the second form is in sarcophagus, facing the approaching sun god and guarded by snakes. The fourth cavern is of Osiris's followers, who are also in sarcophagi and guarded by snakes, ready to meet the sun god. The fifth cavern portrays the headless souls damned to hell. They are called "enemies of Osiris," and their cavern is a prison guarded by three snakes. The sun god will sentence them to a second death.

In the second section of the Book of Caverns, the sun god has entered the Duat. He asks for Osiris to receive him, and his request is granted. Other gods and goddesses in the underworld also receive him in their various forms. The last cavern shows the condemned souls on their way to the Place of Annihilation, the Egyptian concept of hell. Osiris is eager to lead the sun god farther into the cavern, especially where Aker, a gatekeeper of the underworld, is. Aker's gate leads back to Earth, where the sun god has to be by dawn to rise as the sun.

The sun god's journey progresses in the third section of the Book of Caverns. Here, he meets the gods of the sacred Ennead and other deities in the Duat. The condemned souls in the last cavern have reached their destination, the dreadful Place of Annihilation. The souls are hung upside down and are suffering immense punishment for their sins.

In the fourth section of the Book of Caverns, the sun god, Isis, Nephthys, Horus, and Anubis take care of Osiris and protect him. The condemned souls in the last cavern are still suffering at the hands of a ruthless demon, and they are eventually beheaded.

The fifth section portrays the sky goddess Nut, who receives the sun god and raises him up in her arms. Another part of the same section shows Osiris and other gods seeing the sun god off on the final stage of his journey. This is marked by depictions of the rebirth and rejuvenation of Ra. The languishing souls in the lowest caverns are introduced to the next stage of their punishment. Their heads and hearts are set ablaze, and two goddesses are with them in the Place of Annihilation, fanning the flames that slowly and painfully destroy them.

At the end of the sixth section is the sun god's divine barque, the Atet. It is rowed out of the underworld by his entourage with joy, and together, they prepare for the sun god's glorious ascension into the sky.

The Book of Caverns also mentions ten deities of the underworld apart from the known Ammit. These creatures, which are called "minor deities" or "demons," are charged with ensuring the punishment of condemned souls. These vicious demons were portrayed in different sections as fire-spitting snakes, catfish-headed gods, jackal-headed gods, and Ammit. They were all soul predators. A few sections have depictions of Osiris, Nut, and Anubis in the lower caverns, overseeing the punishment of the wicked.

Spine-chilling as the Book of Caverns might be, it represents the reasons why the people of the New Kingdom would have aligned their lives with Ma'at.

The Book of Gates

Just opposite the royal tomb wall of Pharoah Ramesses IV, where the Book of Caverns was discovered, there was a fragment of another ancient text dating to the Middle and New Kingdoms. This text was entitled the Book of Gates by a French Egyptologist named Gaston Maspero.

The Book of Gates portrays a journey through the underworld, but this time through the eyes of mortal souls. Discovered in tombs of kings, nobles, and other bureaucrats, some versions of the Book of Gates were incorrectly sequenced or woven into some content from the *Book of the Dead.*

Pharaoh Seti I's tomb had a colorful and detailed version of this text, showing four men, each of a distinct color of skin, entering the

Duat. This representation of all the races on Earth reinforces the perception of the Duat by the Egyptians as a universal concept. Every human would live on after death, and the only way to get to paradise was to obey Ma'at.

The contents of the complete Book of Gates illustrate the soul's journey through several gates of the Duat and the guardians of each gate. The soul was required to know the name and attributes of each guardian to get past them and continue their journey. The Book of Gates has twelve chapters, each describing an hour of the night and what happens with the souls in each hour.

The first hour is titled "Ushemet-Hatu-Khefti-Ra." It opens with the sun god's arrival in the Duat through Amentet, the Hall of the Horizon. On his divine barque, Ra appears in the form of a scarab beetle, which comes from the creation story of Hermopolis, and he is protected by a snake and two companions named Sia and Hu. The gates of the Duat open, and all the souls of the dead join in welcoming Ra.

In the second hour, titled "Shesat-Makeb-Neb-S," the souls who obeyed Ma'at in their lifetime are separated from the wicked souls. The good souls are in the upper rows of the Book of Gates, and Ra blesses them, saying, "Your offerings are yours, you have power over your cool waters, your souls shall never be hacked to pieces, your meat shall never fail, [you who have] praised [me], and have vanquished Apep for me."

The wicked souls occupy the lower rows, depicted as laying on their backs in punishment. Atum, an aspect of Ra, acts as the son of the sun of god and curses the wicked, saying:

"The word of my father Ra is right (Maat) against you, and my word is right against you...Bound in fetters; your arms shall never more be opened...Your evil deeds [have turned] against you, your plotting [has come] upon you, your abominable acts [have returned] upon you, your destinies are for evil, and your doom has been decreed before Ra; your unjust and perverted judgments are upon yourselves, and the wickedness of your words of cursing are upon you."

The separated souls and the sun god continue down a narrow path until they reach twelve mummified guardian gods at the next entrance.

The third hour, titled "Thentent-Bau," is about crossing a foul-smelling fiery lake. The sun god's barque sails across it unscathed, as do the blessed souls. The wicked souls are burned and scorched by the fire as the beginning of their punishment. The serpent Apophis (Apep) appears at the end of the lake to attack Ra's barque, but Atum and two other gods defeat him.

The fourth hour in the Book of Gates is titled "Urt-Em-Sekhemu-Set." At this time, the traveling souls and the sun god meet the twelve jackal-headed gods guarding the next gates. These gates open to the Lake of Life and the Lake of Uraei. In this realm, the sun god resurrects more dead souls, including that of Osiris, who is protected by his son Horus. At the end of this scene, the souls of the wicked are punished in another bout of fire, and the sojourners arrive at a realm called Arit, whose gates are guarded by twelve gods.

"Sem-her-Ab-Uaa-As" is the name of the fifth hour in the sacred Book of Gates, and in this hour, the sun god and the traveling souls are depicted in a complex series of events. Notably, there is a portrayal of the Hall of Judgment, where the wicked are sent to the Place of Annihilation. In some versions, this sentence is pronounced by Osiris, who sits on his throne. The judgment of souls is linked to the sixth hour, which is titled "Mesperit-Ar-Maat." An array of mummified corpses await resurrection from Ra while armed gods restrain Apophis in this realm.

The seventh hour, "Khesef-Hai-Heseq-Neha-Hra," marks the time when every obstacle to the sun god's rejuvenation for the next dawn is destroyed. Midway through the realm, the sun god assents to the punishment of two of his captured enemies. The blessed souls continue their journey, with one group carrying baskets filled with stalks of grain on their heads. This is a reward for their commitment to Ma'at. The other group each bears the Feather of Truth, an aspect of Ma'at, as a symbol of blessing.

Hour eight is titled "Nesbt-Usha," where time as an infinite element is represented with an endless rope from Aken, the ferryman of the underworld. More blessings are given to the good souls in this realm, while the wicked receive more punishments. The mummies that had waited to be resurrected are gradually coming back to life, and the sun god continues on his barque to the next gate called Aat Shefsheft.

In the ninth hour, "Mak-Neb-S," the sojourners come to a chaotic river representing Nun, in which the souls of many mortals are floating. This does not allude to hopelessness or death. Instead, they will be nourished by the waters and set among the blessed souls to be fed vegetables and bread. The condemned remain in the lowest row; they are still languishing in the fires of destruction at the behest of Horus.

The tenth hour is "Tentenit-Hesq-Khakabu," and it portrays a fierce battle against Apophis, the enemy of Ra. The sun god battles Apophis in different forms, and he is joined by fourteen gods who hold magic-powered nets above their heads. This net is imbued with spells to weaken and defeat Apophis. At the end of this scene is text telling of an upward procession of the sky god. By this point, it is almost morning.

"Sebit-Neb-Uaa-Khesef-Sebiu-Em-Pert-F" is the title of the eleventh hour. Apophis has been defeated, captured, and dismembered. His mutilated body is held in place with a rope, and this time, the lowest row is occupied by gods and goddesses rowing the sun god's barque toward the east for his ascension. Souls of the dead are present to witness the glorious sight.

In the twelfth and final hour of the Book of Gates, the sun god advances to the gates of the final realm, where he is reborn as the bright morning sun. In his company are four gods holding sun disks in their right hands, four gods holding stars in their right hands, four hawk-headed gods holding scepters in their left hands, four ram-headed gods holding scepters in their left hands, one crocodile-headed god holding a serpent in his right hand and a scepter in his left hand, and eight female snake-like creatures holding stars in their left hands. Other details of this scene are the crowns of Ra, a chained Apophis, and four baboons celebrating the rebirth of the sun god.

While Osiris remains in the underworld, the sun god rises from the eastern horizon. The Book of Gates gives an engaging depiction of the Duat, and throughout the twelve hours, the souls traveling with the sun god are consistently enjoined to keep up with the divine barque. Every gate would close after the sun god's barque passed through it, and any soul left behind would be stranded for eternity.

The *Book of the Heavenly Cow*

A popular trope in mythology is the desecration of the world by mankind, leading their creator to be displeased and punish them. The story of Noah's ark and its destruction comes to mind from the Bible, but in Egyptian mythology, it is known as the tale of the Heavenly Cow.

The first version of this book was found in the tomb of the famous Pharaoh Tutankhamun, but it was incomplete. Subsequently, the tombs of Pharaohs Seti I, Ramesses II, and Ramesses III gave whole versions. Historians date this document to the Middle or New Kingdom, and unlike other funerary books, which offer spiritual guidance or depict the realms of the Duat, the *Book of the Heavenly Cow* tells a fascinating story.

The first part, "The Destruction of Mankind," opens with a displeased Ra. He is described as "old, his bones being of silver, and his flesh of gold." Taking advantage of this, humankind has begun plotting a rebellion against their creator. The omniscient Ra summons a council of gods to deliberate on the next course of action. As suggested by Nun, the primordial waters that once covered the earth, Ra sends Hathor, the Eye of Ra, to punish the mortals for their insolence.

From here, the plot weaves into the story of Hathor, where she becomes the bloodthirsty Sekhmet and devours the earth with fire until she is stopped by a strong batch of wine from Ra. This part is called "The Withdrawal of Ra." It is the second part of the story of the Heavenly Cow, and it is linked to the crux of the story, which is titled "The Heavenly Cow."

Ra is determined to return to the sky, far away from his remaining creations. He seeks the help of Nut, the goddess of the sky, and asks to be placed on her back. Nut is confused by the sun god's request and seeks clarity. She then offers herself to be submerged in the magical waters of Nun and transforms into a celestial cow. The sun god mounts the cow and moves upward, just in time for the evil plans of humankind to hatch. In the morning, the people come out in droves, shooting arrows at the escaping sun god, who mocks them, saying, "O slaughterers, may your slaughtering be far removed from me!"

The sun god urges Nut to move faster. She goes higher, and the sun god summons more gods to join her.

Nut, the Heavenly Cow, being helped by the other gods with Ra on top of her.
https://commons.wikimedia.org/wiki/File:Nut1.JPG

Afterward, Ra establishes "The New World Order," which is also the name of the fourth part of the story. Nut becomes the sky and carries the sun (Ra), and Ra creates paradise (the Field of Reeds). Through the magic of Nut and Ra, in the final part, Ma'at is established, and it becomes the responsibility of humankind to uphold it.

The last part of the *Book of the Heavenly Cow* is very significant. In it, the sun god stops coddling his creation. Instead, they are tasked with maintaining the order of the world in exchange for a place in eternal paradise.

Conclusion

In Egyptian mythology, there is almost always a hint of the supernatural. The impact of this on ancient Egypt's history is immense. The people worshiped many gods and goddesses in the Egyptian pantheon. They performed sacred rituals and rites. They celebrated grand festivals, and they conducted elaborate funeral processes. All of these form a major part of Egyptian history.

So far, you have taken an enthralling adventure into the realms of the gods and have seen how their actions affected the humans on Earth and those in the underworld. Although we see myths as stories today, the people back then viewed them as being much more. Relics from the ancient eras of Egypt affirm this. Obelisks, pyramids, mummies, sacred texts, sphinxes, and temples are proof of the magnificent lives of the ancient Egyptian populace and their dedicated belief in something larger than themselves.

While most of them lived regular lives as commoners, they shared the same belief in the afterlife and the fate of all souls, whether they were good or evil. Thus, the people sought to live their lives in accordance with Ma'at in exchange for eternal bliss.

You have read of the ancient Egyptians' efforts and how much they persevered in their lives of worship. Apart from the intentionality of it, a laudable aspect of the ancient Egyptians was how they built those tombs, temples, and other monuments to last forever. Although they were focused on the afterlife, they also thought highly of the future and made sure to leave indestructible evidence of their rich culture behind.

Because of this, Egyptian mythology has been a major contributor to art, history, and popular culture. By the Graeco-Roman era, ancient Egypt had become a melting pot of cultures, with syncretized gods and the construction of new temples. Thousands of years later, Egypt would be occupied by Britain, and the surviving ancient monuments and artifacts would be unearthed.

Every piece of evidence tells stories of the ancient people as written by them. You have read about most of it: the lives of Egyptian gods and goddesses, the creation stories, their myths and folktales, and details of the sacred books. Museums, ancient sites, literature, and film have kept these stories alive for hundreds of years since their discovery. It is not too absurd to say that they will be remembered forever.

Here's another book by Enthralling History that you might like

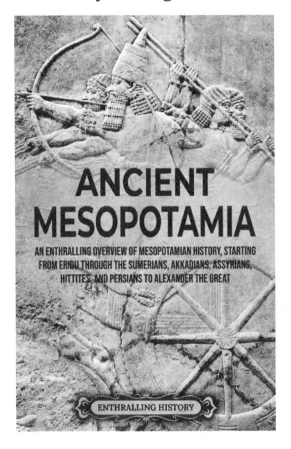

Free limited time bonus

Stop for a moment. We have a free bonus set up for you. The problem is this: we forget 90% of everything that we read after 7 days. Crazy fact, right? Here's the solution: we've created a printable, 1-page pdf summary for this book that you're reading now. All you have to do to get your free pdf summary is to go to the following website: **https://livetolearn.lpages.co/enthrallinghistory/**

Once you do, it will be intuitive. Enjoy, and thank you!

Bibliography

Pinch, G. Egyptian Mythology: A Guide to the Gods, Goddesses, and Traditions of Ancient Egypt. Oxford University Press, 2004.

Bunson, M. *The Encyclopedia of Ancient Egypt.* Gramercy Books, London, 1991.

Shaw, I. *The Oxford History of Ancient Egypt.* Oxford University Press, 2004.

Ikram, S. *Death and Burial in Ancient Egypt.* Longman, 2003.

Leeming, David Adams (2010). *Creation Myths of the World.* Santa Barbaro: ABC-CLIO. p. 102. ISBN 978-1-59884-174-9.

Wallis Budge, E.A. *Egyptian Religion.* Cosimo Classics, 2005.

Wilkinson, R. *The Complete Gods and Goddesses of Ancient Egypt.* Thames & Hudson, 2003.

Hart, George (2004). *Egyptian Myths.* Austin, Texas: University of Texas.

David, R. *Religion and Magic in Ancient Egypt.* Penguin Books, 2002.

M.V., Seton-Williams (1999). *Egyptian Legends and Stories.* U.S.A: Barnes & Noble Publishing.

Nardo, D. *Living in Ancient Egypt.* Thompson/Gale, 2004.

Allen, James P. (2000). *Middle Egyptian: An Introduction to the Language and Culture of Hieroglyphs.* Cambridge University Press.

Robins, G. *The Art of Ancient Egypt.* Harvard University Press, 2008.

Fleming, Fergus; Alan Lothian (1997). *The Way to Eternity: Egyptian Myth.* Amsterdam: Duncan Baird Publishers.

Goelet, O. et. al. *Egyptian Book of the Dead.* Chronicle Books, 2015.

Kemboly, Mpay. 2010. *The Question of Evil in Ancient Egypt.* London: Golden House Publications.

Van De Mieroop, M. *A History of Ancient Egypt.* Wiley-Blackwell, 2007.

Roberts, A. *Hathor Rising: The Power of the Goddess in Ancient Egypt.* Inner Traditions, 1997.

The One and the Many (translated by John Baines, Ithaca, NY: Cornell University Press, 1996).

Strudwick, H. *The Encyclopedia of Ancient Egypt.* Sterling Publishing, 2016.

The Crisis of Polytheism (London: Routledge, 2009).

Della-Piana, Patricia (2010). *Witch Daze, A Perennial Pagan Calendar.*

Quirke, S. (2001). *The Cult of Ra: Sun-worship in Ancient Egypt.* New York: Thames and Hudson, p.144.

"Book of the Dead of Nestanebetisheru."

https://www.britishmuseum.org/collection/object/Y_EA10554-66

"Book of the Dead of Djedkhonsiusankh."

https://www.britishmuseum.org/collection/object/Y_EA10328

Silverman, D. P. *Ancient Egypt.* Oxford University Press, 1997.

Bard, Kathryn (2008) *An Introduction to the Archaeology of Ancient Egypt.*

Herodotus (1920). The Histories with an English translation by A. D. Godley. Cambridge: Harvard University Press. At the Perseus Project of the Tufts University.

Made in the USA
Monee, IL
13 January 2023

25252263R00108